Was Jesus Crazy?

Frédéric Joi

Was Jesus crazy?

Max Milo

© Max Milo Editions
Collection Essais-Documents, Paris, 2024
www.maxmilo.com
ISBN: 978-2-31501-100-1

INTRODUCTION

> "What interests *me* is the psychological type of the Redeemer. He *could well*, in spite of the Gospels, be contained in the Gospels, even if totally mutilated and overloaded with foreign features [...]".
>
> Nietzsche[1]

Jesus is a fascinating being.

He first fascinated some of his contemporaries, in the restricted context of a Jewish country under Roman occupation.

Then he fascinated entire crowds, during his lifetime.

And he was sentenced to death.

But his words and deeds were written, more or less faithfully.

An incredible thing happened: the fascination with Jesus continued through these writings.

Again, he fascinated a few men, then crowds.

---

1. Nietzsche (Friedrich), "L'Antéchrist", in *Œuvres philosophiques complètes*, Paris, Gallimard-NRF, 1990, tome VIII, § 29, p. 188.

In spite of the distance of time and place where he had lived, Jesus continued to fascinate the multitudes. He even fascinated them more and more.

Finally, it has fascinated billions of men for two millennia.

Jesus is a fascinating being.

A Western atheist of the 20th century cannot fail to be surprised. How could Jesus fascinate so many people? If his "Father" does not exist, his claims are all the more absurd. When he claimed to be his son, when he claimed to offer eternity to those who believed in his divinity, or thought he was saving the world by giving his life, etc., all these statements become delusional. What can we say about statements like "I am the bread of life which comes down from heaven"[2], "The Father is in me and I am in the Father"[3], or "He who eats my flesh and drinks my blood has eternal life"[4]?

But Jesus never ceased to maintain that he held the truth, to the point of identifying himself with it:

"I am the way, the truth, and the life."[5]

Insofar as billions of people have taken his claims to be true, the surprised atheist cannot fail to ask a thorny question: how could they be true? Or to turn the question around: how is it that so many people could believe these obviously false claims? All the more so as they are individuals from all times, all places, all origins. Hence this additional question: how can Jesus' statements be universal, so that they can fascinate any man on earth? What does he say that is so captivating that it makes us forget the reality?

---

2. *John* (6:41-42). The quotations from the Bible are taken from the new Geneva edition, translated from the original Hebrew and Greek texts by Louis Segond, version revised in 1975.

3. *John* (14:9-11), see also *John* (16:15).

4. *John* (6:54), see also *Matthew* (26:26-28).

5. *John* (14:6), see also *John* (8:16), (17:19), (18:37).

A Christian could easily account for this fascination: it would emanate from God. The source of Jesus' fascination would have been like the aura of God. However, for the atheist, this explanation does not hold.

The contemporary atheist, who tries to penetrate the double enigma of Jesus' personality and success, encounters another kind of difficulties, more insidious. These are internal difficulties.

In spite of his atheism, the Western atheist remains deeply imbued with Jesus. He is no longer aware of all that is Christian about him. His values are Christian, like peace. His laws are Christian, like monogamy. Its constitution is Christian, like brotherhood. Its language is Christian, like the notion of altruism. Its morals are Christian, like the requirement of modesty or the rejection of vanity. Its temporal references are Christian, like the calendar. Its politeness is Christian, like forgiveness. Its normative judgments are Christian, like the condemnation of suicide. His feelings are Christian, like pity. His ideal is Christian, like charity.

His gaze is distorted by this; especially when observing Jesus himself. The atheist, like the believer, looks at Jesus with his own values. He judges Jesus with his own conclusions. He appreciates Jesus with his own feelings, especially love. He can only see in Jesus a model of Christian values.

Therein lies the main problem of the atheistic Westerner, who unwittingly views reality with the "Jesus glasses", with the viewpoint of Jesus.

The reader of the New Testament, even if he is an atheist, cannot help seeing in Jesus a prophet or a messiah, a founder of religion. He is not at all shocked by the words or actions of Jesus, however abnormal. For example, when Jesus claims to be dealing with "enemies", such as the high religious dignitaries, the Romans or Judas, the reader always takes Jesus' side. They are always the "bad guys," never Jesus. In the end, even without believing in his divinity, history has proven him right.

We look at the world with its values. *A fortiori*, we see him as the personified good. We find it difficult not to attribute to him all the values he preaches, and which are now considered as "qualities".

His values became ours, "therefore" he was right, "therefore" he defended the truth. At worst, the atheist sees him as a wise man. In this case, Jesus' statements are no longer taken literally, but "over-interpreted" as mere metaphors. In particular, whenever Jesus spoke of God, he would have referred to a being that was purely internal to the subject.

It is no small problem for the modern atheist to see Jesus as he was. He must remove the "Christian glasses".

In this sense, a German philosopher of the late NINETEENTH CENTURY IS OF considerable help. Friedrich Nietzsche knows how to go back to the presuppositions of Christianity, to unearth its consequences in our behavior and in our ideas. Thanks to his radical critique of Christianity, he makes it possible to take an extraordinary step back on all these reflexes that we have, every day, without our knowledge. He makes it possible to become aware of the distorting glasses that we wear.

How can Nietzsche achieve this distancing? He shows an unparalleled psychological flair for ferreting out the mental illness beneath the values of Christianity. For example, he guesses, behind the Christian denigration of sexuality, a sad negation of vital instincts, bordering on "melancholy", the old name for depression. By pointing out the insidious disease, Nietzsche leads us to desist from the barely conscious idealization of the first of the Christians.

Nevertheless, however energetic his attacks, Nietzsche stopped short of the source of Christianity. He hardly wrote more than a few pages on the psychology of Jesus[6]. His main contribution, for our subject, lies in the critical distancing of Christianity, which sticks to us so much. He opens the way. But in order to take a further step in the psychological understanding of the Christian religion, the powerful advances of the 20th century are necessary.

Freud took up the critical tone of Nietzsche, and also relied on psychology. However, he devoted his entire life to developing psychology itself. He set up very powerful analysis tools, allowing to go further than Nietzsche's intuition. These new means give a privileged access to what is behind the visible acts or the apparent thoughts of the consciousness. Freudian psychology is like an X-ray of consciousness.

Freud also advanced the psychological understanding of the Christian religion in general, by discovering that believers are obsessive neurotics. This is a decisive advance, allowing the inauguration of a sharp critique.

But Freud, like Nietzsche, did not go up the Christian river to its ultimate source. He devoted only a few incidental paragraphs to Jesus[7].

At least he presented an overview. He showed that psychological analysis could uncover the unconscious thoughts at work in Christianity, especially in its originator. Freud's clues are valuable, and too rare. His work must be continued.

Freudian psychology opens up the possibility of taking off the Christian glasses. It does not judge what is good or bad, but what

---

6. See in particular NIETZSCHE (Friedrich), "L'Antéchrist", in *Œuvres philosophiques complètes*, *op. cit.* Volume VIII, §§ 29-35, pp. 188-195.

7. See in particular FREUD (Sigmund), *Totem and Taboo*, chapter IV, "The infantile return of totemism", in *Complete Works. Psychoanalysis*, Paris, PUF, 1998, part VI, volume XI, p. 374.

is normal or pathological. It makes it possible to distinguish a delusion from a healthy and sensible judgment. It allows us to distinguish between truth and falsehood, which is particularly useful with a character as obsessed with truth as Jesus.

The method of psychology is simple. It focuses on understanding the facts, words and actions of the subject. It starts by identifying his pathological symptoms. Then, from there, it goes back to their cause, like a police investigation. It is then that she brings to light his secret mechanisms, which operate in the unconscious. Nietzsche and Freud made this investigation possible, without carrying it out themselves.

Let us now try to look at Jesus without Christian glasses. Let's try to look at the medical reality, "to see".

CHAPTER I:
THE SCHIZOPHRENIC FEATURES OF JESUS

We seek to explain the success of Jesus, that is, the relationship between a man and a multitude. And since the crowd of believers refers to the Gospels, we will have to do the same. By hypothesis, we will hold them to be "true", in the sense that they must contain, in one way or another, a truth, unnoticed, unconscious. This truth is the key to understanding the glory of a man.

According to these texts, Jesus often seemed to show a certain tendency to isolate himself. Many passages even describe him as shunning the crowds. This behavior contrasts with the fact that he was otherwise able to captivate them.

"Towards morning, while it was still very dark, he got up and went out to a deserted place, where he prayed."[8]

Sometimes Jesus had a more radical behavior, which makes his glory even more inexplicable:

"When he had sent them [the crowd] away, he went out to the mountain to pray. When evening came, the boat [where his

---

8. *Mark* (1:35), see also *Matthew* (14:13), *Mark* (1:45), *Luke* (4:42), (5:16).

disciples were] was in the middle of the sea, and Jesus was alone on land."[9]

He avoided the crowd, even when, to top it all off, they came to grant him power as king of the Jews:

"And Jesus, knowing that they were coming to take him away to make him king, withdrew again to the mountain, he alone."[10]

The Gospels feel the need to explain this attitude of reclusion by recourse to God. This concern for explanation already underlines in itself an originality of Jesus' way of life.

"Immediately the Spirit drove Jesus into the wilderness, where he spent forty days being tempted by Satan."[11]

More realistic contemporaries would probably note that Jesus had not begun his public ministry until he was about thirty. Before that, he may have spent a period of asceticism among the Essenes, a type of monk of the time. In this case, Jesus' taste for solitude would only be a cultural achievement. Nevertheless, this pragmatic explanation can at best only justify the reinforcement of a tendency to isolation, which had appeared since Jesus' childhood. In view of the limited information available about his youth, the following clue is all the more valuable:

"When he was twelve years old, [Jesus and his family] went up [to Jerusalem] according to the custom of the feast. Then, when the days were over and they returned, the child Jesus remained in Jerusalem. His father and mother did not notice."[12]

Sometimes he would bring a few friends along in his solitude:

"Jesus took Peter, James, and John, his brother, and led them away to a high mountain."[13]

---

9. *Mark* (6:46-47), see also *Matthew* (14:23).
10. *John* (6:15).
11. *Mark* (1:12), see also *Matthew* (4:1) and *Luke* (4:1-2).
12. *Luke* (2: 42-43).
13. *Matthew* (17:1), see also *Mark* (9:2).

The explanation that Jesus would have given to this curious personality trait would have been contained in his famous sentence:

"My kingdom is not of this world [...]"[14]

In his mind, this implied that his kingdom resided in heaven. However, without God or heaven, what could that kingdom be? Where did he intend to isolate himself?

The condition for being able to do without others to this extent is to be self-sufficient. Precisely, Jesus seemed to develop what can be called an "inflated ego". Reading between the lines of the Texts, he seemed to be very interested in his own person. He talked a lot about himself, about what was going to happen to him, about who he thought he was, etc. He showed a great deal of confidence in his own abilities and in the ability of others to help him. He showed great confidence in his own statements, which he always presented as truths ("I tell you the truth").

This ego was evident in the way he made everything about himself.

"He who hears you hears me, and he who rejects you rejects me; and he who rejects me rejects him who sent me."[15]

If Jesus is the son of God, this sentence is not surprising. If not, then he thought he was everywhere, and that everything concerned him.

It is striking to see, through a revealing prediction, to what extent Jesus believed himself to be at the center of everyone's interests:

"When the Son of Man comes in his glory, with all the angels, he will sit on the throne of his glory. All nations will be gathered before him."[16]

---

14. *John* (18:36).
15. *Luke* (10:16).
16. *Matthew* (25:31-32).

CHAPTER I: THE SCHIZOPHRENIC FEATURES OF JESUS

This is just one of many instances. Jesus always gave the impression that everything had to revolve around him - which would be perfectly normal if he were the son of God.

In addition to this self-interest and his tendency to isolate himself, another personality trait seems to thicken the mystery of Jesus, apparently predestining him even less to convince the crowds. His language was obscure, which should have led to an obvious communication problem.

It is well known that Jesus used parables. A parable is an allegorical story from the holy books under which a moral or religious teaching is hidden[17]. To speak in parables is to speak in a roundabout, enigmatic way. An allegory, on the other hand, is a narrative that uses concrete elements coherently. Each element of the allegory is used as a symbol. The symbol designates a concrete entity (a sign, a character, an object), which represents an abstract value, by tacit convention. But Jesus invented his images, unusual and striking, which no tacit convention allowed to decipher simply.

Jesus certainly did not create the principle of parables. Solomon, in particular, had already produced many of them. However, Jesus' personality was strongly marked by this great inventiveness in the art of expressing indirectly, by a sometimes complex metaphor, a religious injunction. To review all his metaphorical inventions would be tedious. But one or two cases, somewhat convoluted, are enough to highlight this particularity.

"Salt is a good thing; but if salt loses its flavor, what will you season it with? It is not good for the earth, nor for the manure; it is thrown out. He who has ears to hear, let him hear."[18]

"No one who lights a lamp covers it with a vessel or puts it under a bed, but puts it on a lampstand, so that those who enter

---

17. *See* Le Grand Robert.
18. *Luke* (14:34-35).

16

may see the light. For there is nothing hidden that should not be discovered, nothing secret that should not be known and brought to light. Take heed, therefore, how you hear; for to him who has shall be given, but to him who has not shall be taken away even that which he thinks he has."[19]

Why was Jesus so enamored of parables? How can we discover the unambiguous meaning of each of them? The history of controversies on these questions seems to indicate that the task is impossible. Already in his lifetime, Jesus caused misunderstandings and misinterpretations:

"The Jews said, 'It took forty-six years to build this temple, and you will raise it up in three days. But he spoke of the temple of his body."[20]

The disciples came to him and said, "Why do you speak to them in parables? Why do you speak to them in parables?"[21]

The obscurity of these metaphors is obvious, since Jesus himself had to explain their meaning:

"He spoke to them in many such parables, as they were able to hear him. He did not speak to them without a parable; but he explained everything to his disciples in particular."[22]

Jesus' words, besides being enigmatic, were supposed to have an effect on material reality. There is a clear tendency to believe in the supernatural here, attributing to the word a power that it does not possess.

"[On a boat shaken by the waves and the wind:] Being awakened, he threatened the wind, and said to the sea, Silence!"[23]

---

19. *Luke* (8:16-18).
20. *John* (2:21).
21. *Matthew* (13:3, 10).
22. *Mark* (4: 33-34).
23. *Mark* (4:39).

A famous passage confirms this same trait, in a dramatic and supposedly metaphorical way:

"Truly I say to you, if anyone says to this mountain, 'Get up from there and throw yourself into the sea,' and does not doubt in his heart, but believes that what he says is happening, he will see it fulfilled. Therefore I say to you, whatever you ask in prayer, believe that you have received it, and you will see it fulfilled."[24] Even though the modern believer, a little ashamed of such a superstition, would like to see only images, among the materials of these parables, the unconscious recognizes its own! Dreams attest to these fantasies of superpower over the material world.

Jesus did not invent many of the supernatural beliefs that he conveyed. But he occasionally embellished his speeches with superstitions of his own:

"But when you are delivered up, do not worry about how you will speak or what you will say: what you have to say will be given to you in that very hour; for it is not you who will speak, but the Spirit of your Father who will speak in you."[25]

Finally, other strange traits defined Jesus' personality, precisely about his identity...

Who was Jesus? This is a particularly difficult question, which can only be answered by a long investigation. But interestingly enough, Jesus' own answer to this question was anything but unequivocal.

To begin with, he often spoke about himself in the third person, which is in itself a crucial clue.

"[Speaking of himself] They will sentence him to death [...] and on the third day he will rise again."[26]

---

24. *Mark* (11:22-24), see also *Matthew* (21:21-22).
25. *Matthew* (10:19-20).
26. *Matthew* (20:19).

To further confuse the issue, this third person did not always refer to the same person. Sometimes he let himself be called "king". This was probably metaphorical, since a famous person already existed, Herod, who held the position of king of the Jews.

Pilate asked him, "Are you the King of the Jews? Jesus answered, "You say so."[27]

At times he called himself "Son of Man", a curious expression that he did not invent, and which poses a problem:

"For the Son of Man is to come in the glory of his Father, with his angels [...]"[28]

Sometimes he claimed an identity between himself and the Father[29]... In this case his dialogues with himself, during his frequent prayers, must have taken on an unusual dimension. Unless one accepts the idea that he was really the son of God, how can one explain this kind of puzzling assertion?

Who was he talking to in his mind? How many interlocutors were there in his mind? Did he know it himself? Christians will then evoke the famous "Trinity", and will themselves admit to what extent it was shrouded in mystery. What does it mean to be "three in one", or "one in three"? What is a Father, a Son and, even more, an amazing "Holy Spirit"?

Finally, it should not be surprising that his relatives, especially those who had seen him grow up, called him crazy:

"The parents of Jesus, when they heard what was going on, came to seize him; for they said, 'He is out of his mind. [That is, he is mad as a hatter]"[30]

It was this poor reception by his own family that made him pronounce the famous sentence:

---

27. *Mark* (15:2), see also *John* (18:37) and *Matthew* (27:11).
28. *Matthew* (16:27).
29. *John* (14:9-11), see also *John* (16:15).
30. *Mark* (3:21).

"I tell you the truth, no prophet is well received in his own country."[31]

And the crowd itself was divided. If one part was convinced by his assertions, the other remained much less willing:

"Why do you seek to kill me? The crowd answered, "You have a demon. [Translation: You are crazy]"[32]

Jesus appears more and more difficult to define. The equivocal message that he delivered about his own identity should not *a priori* simplify the explanation of his success. From the very beginning, the character of Jesus is disconcerting because of several symptoms which, although visible, seem no less heterogeneous.

These scattered traits, developed alone, would not necessarily be pathological. But when they are combined in the same subject, they are the mark of a certain mental illness. A double characteristic movement seemed to animate Jesus: on the one hand, a tendency to withdraw into oneself, and on the other hand, an irrepressible need to invent an imaginary universe, hermetic, abstract and difficult to communicate. This phenomenon is specific to schizophrenia. The schizophrenic withdraws from the world and builds another one instead, in his head.

This withdrawal is a sign of "autism", from the Greek "auto", which means "self" (as opposed to another). In children, whose symptoms are not yet organized or intellectualized, autism is often the main pathological manifestation. It consists of isolation, a break in relations with the environment, and withdrawal into oneself.

In the adult schizophrenic, a "psychic dissociation" is added, where the different compartments of the individual's life become sickly disjointed. His gestures are no longer in phase with his

---

31. *Luke* (4:24).
32. *John* (7:19-20).

thoughts, which are themselves no longer in phase with his emotions. These three compartments, which normally unfold at the same time, become somehow independent, disjointed, "dissociated" according to the accepted term. A gesture of prostration can accompany ideas of grandeur, and the whole can be completed by a great emotional coldness. This dissociation can go as far as a dislocation of the personality, with several identities for the same individual, which intervene in turn or simultaneously.

Finally, schizophrenia is characterized by delusional and unorganized outbursts. The schizophrenic has false ideas that are disconnected from reality. He or she utters nonsensical words, but does not act on them. Nor does he try to develop them logically, with arguments based on reality. The schizophrenic in the waking state behaves as in a dream, without logic.

Schizophrenia is a serious psychological illness, and medical research is struggling to understand how it works, not to mention the difficulties in treating it. To account for its psychological mechanism, one explanation dominates today. It is due to Freud, who developed it from a first sketch by his disciple Abraham[33].

Here is the basis: "The process of repression itself consists of a detachment of the libido from persons - and things - previously loved."[34] The sexual impulses (libido), after having attached themselves to other individuals, return to the subject himself,

---

33. ABRAHAM (Karl), *The psychosexual differences between hysteria and dementia praecox*, 1908, see note 2 p. 292 of the "Remarques psychanalytiques sur un cas de paranoïa", *in* FREUD (Sigmund), *Œuvres complètes. Psychanalyse*, Paris, PUF, 1993, volume X, as well as LAGACHE (Daniel), (under the direction of), LAPLANCHE (Jean) and PONTALIS (Jean-Bertrand), *Vocabulaire de la psychanalyse*, Paris, PUF, coll. "Bibliothèque de psychanalyse", 1990, p. 262.

34. FREUD (Sigmund), "Psychoanalytical remarks on a case of paranoia (*Dementia paranoides*) described in autobiographical form", ("The Schreber case", written in 1910, published in 1911), in *Œuvres complètes. Psychoanalysis*, Paris, PUF, 1993, volume X, p. 294.

in a backward movement. The patient loses interest in external reality and focuses most of his interest on himself. He diverts his impulses to his own benefit. This is a meaning of the word "repression" that is different from the usual meaning (usually, it concerns neuroses and means "to push a representation back into the unconscious"). We will speak of "reflux".

More generally, schizophrenia belongs to the group of psychoses, which also includes paranoia. As such, it is opposed to the neuroses. Freud characterized these two families in a clear way. A minimum of technical vocabulary appears necessary to understand this characterization.

In psychosis, the "I", in the service of the "id", withdraws from a part of reality, rejects it and reconstructs another universe, imaginary, by the delirium and the hallucination[35].

The ego designates the subject. The id refers to the subject's unconscious, containing in particular his drives and his repressed past. Freud distinguishes two main types of drives: the life drive (hunger, sexuality, survival instinct, love, etc.) and the death drive (destructive or murderous desires, hate, etc.). "Reality" refers to society, others, and the laws that govern society.

In other words, the subject rejects society, without recognizing its rules. He refuses others, in favor of his own unconscious impulses, like a serial killer who ignores the laws, in order to directly satisfy his murderous desires.

Then, after having withdrawn his interest from the world, the psychotic reconstructs it in himself. To describe this phenomenon, Freud quotes lines from Goethe:

"Woe! Woe!

You destroyed it,

---

35. FREUD (Sigmund), "The loss of reality in neurosis and psychosis", 1924, in *Œuvres complètes. Psychoanalysis*, Paris, PUF, 1994, volume XVII, p. 37.

This beautiful world,
With a powerful fist!
It collapses, it collapses!
A demigod smashed it! [...]
Powerful
Among the sons of the earth,
More splendid
Rebuild it,
In your bosom, re-edit it!"[36]

This reconstruction is internal, it is carried out in imagination, by "delirium" and "hallucination". The psychotic imagines, invents and reconstructs reality in his imagination, like a dream.

But dreams are constituted from the unconscious of the subject, his id. It is the same for this universe reinvented by the psychotic. The schizophrenic dreams awake. He acts like a person who watches the day fall through the window. After sunset, he sees only his own image, reflected through the glass, of the interior of the house. Instead of reality, he sees only the reflection of his interiority. The schizophrenic does not nourish any more interest for the external world.

Thus, in their principle, the delirious images that appear in the reinvented universe of the psychotic are constructed from his own unconscious. Such is the imaginary, metaphorical and fabulist material that feeds the parables.

Let us now analyze the symptoms of Jesus, found in the New Testament, with the help of Freudian psychology.

Jesus' first symptom, social isolation, was concomitant with his rejection of the crowd, both of which were linked to the curious claim that his kingdom was elsewhere. Jesus undoubtedly

---

36. *Faust*, part I, verses 1607-1612 and 1617-1621, quoted *in* FREUD (Sigmund), *Complete works. Psychoanalysis, op. cit.* Volume X, p. 293.

withdrew some of his impulses from the world and brought them back to himself. This pendulum effect produces a swelling of his ego, as well as the construction of an internal universe, a "kingdom", from his unconscious. Under these conditions, it is no longer surprising that Jesus could believe himself to be at the center of everyone's interests. He placed himself at the center of his own interests, he whose ego constituted an entire universe. He could only report any event outside himself.

Then comes the delicate question of the symbolism at work in his parables. It is understandable that a word should designate an object other than the one to which it usually refers. However, Jesus did not specify the new objects to which he was only alluding, in the "second degree". This second meaning, which Jesus must have had in mind, is far from a consensus. How is this possible? And how can we get to the meaning that Jesus was definitely lending to these parables?

The problem is twofold. First, Jesus was inventing new symbols. At the time of his invention, there was no convention for deciphering them. Second, different men, living at different times, dragged these symbols into a whirlwind of divergent interpretations, depending on the different social conventions of Christian history. A host of speculations remained possible. Endless divergences followed one another in history, especially with the religious schisms, heresies, the many Christian currents, the different churches, etc.

Through the ages, however, and even without understanding this second meaning, which Jesus must have been thinking about, the listeners remained fascinated. It was as if his allusive statements had contained an unchanging, albeit underlying, meaning. What remains fundamentally unchanged in Jesus' parables, beyond all the successive interpretations that have been made of them?

24

A hypothesis could open up an explanation right now, at least in principle, even if it means supporting it only afterwards with duly analyzed examples. A third sense would exist, or rather a sense of degree zero. It is the sense of the unconscious. A word or an expression used by Jesus probably alluded to his own unconscious. This meaning, which he himself did not know, concerned only his mental interiority. Jesus was content to say it, by "inspiration". He considered it important to state it, without taking into account social conventions or its understanding by others. Sometimes it was understandable, sometimes not. But always it was a reference to his own unconscious, without his or his listener's knowledge. Jesus let himself be guided above all by his delusional intuition.

This is why, in this book, the parables will be taken not so much in the first degree, as in the zero degree, deliberately leaving aside the always debatable "second degree". Case-by-case explanations can only be attempted later on, as many other mechanisms are still necessary to access this unconscious meaning. For the moment, let us stick to the hypothesis that the meaning of the parables was an involuntary allusion to Jesus' unconscious.

His strange language was also the result of a rejection of the usual conventions of communication, of the social reality of his time.

The problem remains of knowing why the unconscious of Jesus could interest others than himself. What was so special about the unconscious functioning of this man?

His belief in supernatural phenomena remains to be explained, whether or not it is shared by his contemporaries. From the point of view of psychology, it is commonplace to see a psychotic giving credence to unreal laws. He has withdrawn not only from reality, but also from the natural laws that govern it, to the benefit of his interiority, which is governed by other laws.

CHAPTER I: THE SCHIZOPHRENIC FEATURES OF JESUS

The latter can be said to be supernatural if their origin is attributed to heaven, that world above nature. However, psychology requires that they be attributed to the unconscious. In dreams, many acts become possible that are not in reality: flying in the air, breathing under water, or moving objects at a distance. It is an old fantasy of humanity, an archaic way of thinking, which consists in dreaming awake.

The dream also ignores the principle of identity. The same character can represent others, or even metamorphose into other people. Everyone has experienced that the dreamer can see himself from the outside, as another subject, as a "he. Jesus acted in this way, in the waking state. The Trinity appears as a direct representation of these curious dream splits, which seem to be able to go as far as three times in an exceptional case. But what can we say about a person who would push this unhealthy logic to the point of continuing to believe in these nocturnal wanderings in the broad daylight of consciousness, and wanting to convince his listeners?

In severe cases, a schizophrenic may have been autistic from childhood, in which case he withdrew his affection from those around him at a very early age. He has not been able to construct his identity correctly, which is normally shaped by the natural identification of children with their environment, in particular their parents. This identification deficit generates a floating identity in adulthood.

Jesus could speak of himself as "I" as well as "he," or he could claim to speak for God. His prayers in the wilderness were likely to take the form of internal conversations, which excluded reality. In these internal dialogues, the roles were probably not as well determined as they are in a healthy person. At least two people were probably present. But "who was who?" must have remained quite indeterminate. At least the dogma of the Trinity had the merit to fix some limit to these identity floats. A schizophrenic Trinity.

That Jesus was considered a madman during his lifetime is no longer surprising, whether in front of his own family or in front of a part of the crowd. Schizophrenia is not insignificant, even if Jesus only borrows certain traits from this psychological illness.

Many problems remain to be faced. If Jesus had been a mere fabulator, eccentric and isolated, he would never have seduced the crowds. The vast majority of schizophrenics communicate little or poorly, and are quickly taken for madmen by those close to them, even without the slightest knowledge of psychology on their part. However, during his lifetime, only his family and part of the crowd became aware of his madness. The other part believed in him.

Jesus could not be simply schizophrenic. He had to be much more.

We would like to find out what.

Chapter II:
The Analogue Character of Jesus

From what we can gather from the Gospels, Jesus seemed to be very binary. He seemed to like to divide the universe into two distinct parts, contrary to a reality that knows many nuances. He was probably what has since been called "Manichean". This way of seeing things can be seen in many passages of the Gospels[37]:

"Every good tree bears good fruit, but the bad tree bears bad fruit. A good tree cannot bear bad fruit, or a bad tree bear good fruit."[38]

This division with an axe came back even for a serious question, the balance of a life. The following statement is striking, so much it seems that in an existence, a man accomplishes acts sometimes "good" and sometimes "bad"...

"Those who have done good will rise to life, but those who have done evil will rise to judgment."[39]

Finally, this infantile vision of the world appears in the formula:

---

37. See especially *Matthew* (6:24), (12:36), (15:11), *Luke* (16:13).
38. *Matthew* (7:17-18).
39. *John* (5:29).

"He who is not with me is against me [...]".[40]

This binary split is repeated with the question of truth. Jesus kept repeating that he was right, that he held the truth, while the others would always be wrong. Rarely has a man been more certain of his facts. His formula "in truth" is edifying in this respect. He repeated it over and over again, sometimes doubling it, sometimes adding to it - "Truly, truly, I say to you".

"I was born and came into the world to give testimony to the truth. Whoever is of the truth hears my voice."[41]

Most of the time, his argument was simple. This truth was supposed to come from God:

"I can do nothing of myself: according to what I hear, I judge; and my judgment is right, because I do not seek my own will, but the will of him who sent me."[42]

In a world without God, this is a mystery to be unraveled: how could Jesus remain so certain of holding a truth of divine origin? Where did his incredible conviction come from?

This certainty of being right had its opposite consequence:

"You are in error, because you do not understand either the Scriptures or the power of God."[43]

In the same vein, he did not suffer to be contradicted:

"After Jesus said that he was going to die] And Peter, having taken him aside, began to rebuke him. But Jesus, turning and looking at his disciples, rebuked Peter, and said, Get thee behind me, Satan: for thou knowest not the things of God, thou hast only human thoughts."[44]

---

40. *Matthew* (12:30), see also *Mark* (9:40) and *Luke* (9:50), (11:23).
41. *John* (18:37), see also *John* (8:16), (14:6), (17:19).
42. *John* (5:30), see also *Mark* (9:4-8), *John* (7:28, 30), (8:13-14), (8:40), (8:54-55).
43. *Matthew* (22:29), see also *Mark* (12:24-25), (12:27), *Luke* (23:34).
44. *Mark* (8:32-33), see also *Luke* (9:59-62), (21:15).

More generally, Jesus seems to have always been convinced that he had the truth, and no one was ever able to change his mind. Even in the face of the threat of imminent death, he maintained his convictions. It was a stubbornness that lasted all his life. Jesus was without doubt one of the most uninfluential men the world has ever seen.

According to the Gospels, it would seem that this very orderly representation of things, and this omnipresent certainty, was accompanied in Jesus by a certain interest in cleanliness, which guided some of his images:

"There is nothing outside of man that can defile him when it enters him, but what comes out of man is what defiles him."[45]

Jesus used the notion of purity extensively, on a moral level. On the one hand, he distinguished between the so-called "unclean" spirits, metaphorically linked to evil. And, in contrast, Jesus himself presented himself as a "pure" spirit, who "washed away" faults (through forgiveness). Although he did not invent this rhetoric, it did please him.

"Blessed are the pure in heart, for they shall see God!"[46]

Sometimes, paradoxically, Jesus could disregard basic rules of politeness or cleanliness:

"A Pharisee asked him to dine with him. He went in and sat down to dinner. The Pharisee saw with astonishment that he had not washed before the meal."[47]

Jesus seemed to have an obsession with money matters. This interest is a trait of his character that often goes unnoticed because it was indirect. Jesus probably never sought personal wealth. His

---

45. *Mark* (7:15), see also *Matthew* (15:11).
46. *Matthew* (5:8), see also *Luke* (11:41).
47. *Luke* (11:37-38).

CHAPTER II: THE ANALOGUE CHARACTER OF JESUS

influence on the crowds would have allowed him to do so. This paradox is one more mystery to be solved.

First of all, Jesus made much of the relationship between the rich and the poor, implicitly attributing a great deal of importance to money, even with a negative connotation:

"A rich man's land had yielded much." [But God said to him, "Foolish man, this very night your soul will be required of you; and what you have prepared, for whom will it be? So it is with him who stores up treasures for himself, and is not rich for God."[48]

Secondly, and more importantly, his parables often used the image of commercial exchange, even to evoke such sacred events as the entrance to paradise.

"Jesus said to him, 'If you want to be perfect, go, sell what you have and give it to the poor, and you will have treasure in heaven.'"[49]

In the social context of Jesus' time, commerce was so important that it does not seem to be original. However, Jesus makes full use of this aspect of human relations in his way of expressing himself. The fact that it is a commonplace personality trait for the time does not prevent it from being... a personality trait, the psychological meaning of which remains to be found.

Understanding what is the "anal character", also called "obsessive personality", is crucial to decipher the meaning of these curious specificities of behavior and expression, without resorting to the existence of God.

It is a well-structured personality, marked by a constant concern for order and cleanliness, a great meticulousness, a rigorous punctuality and a certain perfectionism. It also includes a strong stubbornness, which accounts for the tenacity, the perseverance of these subjects who are not easily influenced and are

---

48. *Luke* (12:16-21).
49. *Matthew* (19:21), see also *Luke* (12:33), (18:22).

willingly authoritarian. In the moral field, these characteristics are expressed in the fidelity to commitments, the scrupulous attitude in obligations, the sense of duty[50].

Freud explains that these personality traits are reaction formations against the pleasures taken in early childhood at the sadistic-anal stage[51]. The child goes through several stages, several steps, during which certain parts of his body constitute privileged sources of pleasure.

Watching the children is enough to realize this.

The baby concentrates his activity on the mouth, with sucking, which provides food and well-being. He brings everything to the mouth. This is the "oral stage".

From about the age of three, a big change occurs. The young child has to face the daunting task of controlling his excrement. The anus becomes the center of attention for the little child, who takes great pleasure in controlling his or her bowel movements. The child is encouraged to do this by the adults around him. When he succeeds in going in the potty, he arouses great joy in the adults. He feels like he is giving them a gift. He has to learn to be clean, which is contrary to the great satisfaction he gets from messing up his environment, smearing his food, etc. He also likes to break, destroy and dismantle. He also likes to break, destroy and disobey. This is the moment when a crisis of his aggressive impulses occurs. He learns swear words with a formidable efficiency, which he takes great pleasure in repeating.

This stage of infantile development is called, logically enough, "sadistic-anal stage".

---

50. See LEMPERIÈRE (Thérèse) and FÉLINE (André) *et al, Psychiatrie de l'adulte*, Paris, Masson, 1995, chapter XI, "Les personnalités pathologiques", pp. 126-127.
51. See FREUD (Sigmund), "Caractère et érotisme anal", 1908, in *Névrose, psychose et perversion*, Paris, PUF, 1992, pp. 143-148.

However, in the unconscious, nothing that has been experienced disappears. The desires, once felt, continue to exist, but only in the unconscious, since society prevents their realization.

This is how the anal character is born. When these sadistic-anal impulses are too active in the unconscious, the subject reacts by giving himself opposite habits and duties. Excessive cleanliness appears as a reactionary formation against this taste for dirtiness, just as exaggerated submission and politeness are substituted for intense unconscious aggression. Sometimes the repressed impulses are expressed directly, with tyrannical attitudes, foul language or other violations of the rules of propriety. Some urges may also be "sublimated," that is, they may take on symbolic forms that are socially useful or accepted. The appetite for money replaces the child's interest in his or her feces. In this sense, money is a universal symbol, with a meaning other than that consciously given by Jesus or his listeners.

After the sadistic-anal stage, comes the "phallic" stage, during which the child finds a new source of pleasure with his sex, the penis or the clitoris. This is the age when the child does not stop touching his genitals, which is opposed by the necessary educational environment. These three stages disappear then, at the end of childhood, to give place to a "stage of latency". However, they marked forever the unconscious, and reappear simultaneously with the puberty...

The personality traits of Jesus, mentioned in this chapter, can now be explained, with the exception of his aggressiveness, which will be dealt with in the next chapter.

Jesus' character seems to have been built in reaction to strong sadistic-anal impulses, hence his exaggerated concern for order. This appeared in several forms: an obsessive duty of purity and a certain authoritarianism. This order and this purity appeared directly in this famous binary, clear-cut, Manichean judgment, which left no room for nuances or approximations. This binary classification was operated in force, which still betrays the authoritarianism, of sadistic origin. The infantile pleasure of holding back and controlling one's bowel movements finally broke through in Jesus' manifest stubbornness. Not being able to tolerate contradiction, or being convinced that he was always right, meant aggressively imposing his vision of the world order, against natural or social laws.

As with schizophrenia, this order is derived from the unconscious, and necessarily conflicted with the reality of the society of his time. Jesus rejected the social order of reality, as a psychotic. He also sought to impose another order, not from God, as he believed, but from his unconscious.

This hypersensitivity to order presents two contradictory aspects, as a double movement reversed from schizophrenia. On the one hand, Jesus rejected any external authority that did not abound in the direction of his personal desires. On the other hand, he tried to impose a new order, his own. Jesus was both orderly, as far as his own design was concerned, and disorderly, in that he liked to destroy or defile any order that did not emanate from himself. In concrete terms, he demanded purity with regard to the rules he imposed, while he could be willing to be dirty and rude with regard to the laws of others. In this case, the repressed impulse pierces directly, which is typical of the anal character.

This usually includes three characteristics, which are order-liness (along with cleanliness), stubbornness and... greed. Jesus was more concerned with what he called truth or justice than with getting rich. There was no evidence that he was stingy or venal. On the contrary, Jesus constantly urged the abandonment of earthly riches.

On the other hand, if he really believed in this wealth of heaven, which would surpass all earthly treasures, then his lack of appetite for material money must be transposed, as well as his hatred of the rich. Didn't he think he held the key to the kingdom of God? Jesus became *ipso facto* very rich himself.

Sublimation" refers to a psychological mechanism that redirects basic impulses towards higher, socially valued interests. If money represents a sublimation of the infantile interest in excrement, Jesus sublimated it a second time, by being more interested in heaven than in material goods. The object remains the same, as a commodity that can bring pleasure and accumulate. However, if paradise does not exist, it is no longer above, towards heaven, that Jesus' primary interest points. It is below, in the unconscious. Jesus had an obsession with wealth that was no longer heavenly, but unconscious. This wealth, which fascinated him so much and which he constantly promised to his listeners, suddenly takes on a completely different aspect...

Now a very special class of psychotics is emerging. They arise at the confluence of anal retentiveness, with its great concern for order, and schizophrenia, with its inflated ego and disorganized delusional outbursts. These particular psychotics are rare in the population, although they cause great social agitation.

From there to understand how a psychotic with an anal character could meet the slightest success with the crowds, by producing convoluted images from his infantile desires, the road is still long.

Chapter III: The Paranoia of Jesus

Against all expectations, Jesus seemed particularly aggressive, both in his words and in his actions. He had clearly announced the color, on several occasions:

"Do not think that I have come to bring peace on earth; I have not come to bring peace, but a sword. For I have come to put division between man and his father, between daughter and mother, between daughter-in-law and mother-in-law; and a man's enemies will be those of his own household."[52]

Let us assume that this proclamation is, once again, a metaphor. Let us imagine that Jesus had in mind only mental wars, moral combats, choices of values. The unconscious is not mistaken, the image used remains a warlike image, the most aggressive. The symbol of the sword leaves little doubt. Moreover, the previous quote was perhaps an allusion to his own family, who did not believe in him. Whether this is the case or not, wanting to bring war to a family betrays a very intense aggressiveness.

---

52. *Matthew* (10:34-36), (24:6), see also *Luke* (12:49-53).

Jesus seemed to want to impose his point of view by force, even if it was metaphorical:

"Behold, I have given you power to tread on serpents and scorpions, and over all the power of the enemy; and nothing shall by any means hurt you."[53]

Where is the great pacifist?

Another form of aggressiveness, indirect this one but not less obvious, is represented by authoritarianism, not to say tyranny. This in turn can take many forms, including a strong propensity to give orders to everyone, and preferably orders that are very difficult to carry out. Jesus seemed to excel in this form of aggressiveness.

If God existed, and if Jesus was his messenger, it would certainly be banal to see him constantly giving orders. If God does not exist, it becomes very problematic to explain why Jesus spent his time tyrannizing those around him with his countless injunctions. How can we explain that he allowed himself to tell everyone what to do, clearly positioning himself as a righter of wrongs?

This is the time to think about taking off your Christian glasses: even an atheist could believe that this aggressiveness was justified, with the unintentional idea that Jesus was in the right. His commandments may be considered "good" today, but they are still commandments, to be received as such. The fact that his values have since been imposed does not detract from the formal authoritarianism with which Jesus tried to inflict them, quite the contrary.

Jesus gave orders to some:

"Go away; behold, I send you out like lambs in the midst of wolves. Carry no purse, no bag, no shoes, and greet no one on the way. In whatever house you enter, first say, 'Peace be upon

___

53. *Luke* (10:19).

this house. And if there is a child of peace there, your peace shall rest upon him; if not, it shall return to you. Stay in that house, eating and drinking what you are given, for the worker deserves his wages. Do not go from house to house. Into whatever city you enter, and they do not receive you, go into its streets and say to them, 'The kingdom of God has come near you. But into whatsoever city ye enter, and they receive you not, go ye into the streets thereof, and say: We shake off the very dust of your city from under our feet [...]"[54]

Jesus was giving orders to the crowd:

"Now there were about five thousand men. Jesus said to his disciples, "Have them sit down in rows of fifty."[55]

Jesus gave orders to the spirits:

Jesus said to him, "Get out, Satan!"[56]

Jesus gave universal commands, which were particularly demanding:

"If your right eye causes you to stumble, pluck it out and throw it from you. [... And if your right hand is a stumbling block to you, cut it off and throw it away from you..."[57]

On this last point, the reader of the Gospels will be able to answer, once again, that these are only symbols, metaphors, allegories, in short simple parables. It is not so obvious, however, to see certain populations, at certain times, cutting off the hands of thieves, or the tongues of liars. From symbol to reality, the way is short. Then, the true referent of this symbol remains to be discovered...

---

54. *Luke* (10:2-11), see also *Matthew* (4:18-19), (12:15-16), (22:37-40), (23:26), *Mark* (6:7-9), (12:29-31, 34), (14:38), *Luke* (9:1-5), *John* (1:43)
55. *Luke* (9:14), see also *Matthew* (11:28-29).
56. *Matthew* (4:10).
57. *Matthew* (5:29), (6:7-9), see also *John* (13:34).

Jesus' tyranny, a sign of his aggressiveness, could also take a negative form. Instead of ordering what should be done, Jesus took pleasure in limiting people's scope of action with a myriad of prohibitions of all kinds.

Jesus imposed prohibitions on some:

"If you want to enter life, keep the commandments. Which ones?" he said to him. And Jesus answered: "You shall not kill; you shall not commit adultery; you shall not steal; you shall not bear false witness; honor your father and mother; and love your neighbor as yourself: You shall love your neighbor as yourself."[58]

Jesus imposed prohibitions on the crowd:

"Do not fear those who kill the body and after that can do nothing more. I will show you whom you should fear."[59]

Jesus imposed universal prohibitions:

"[...] Be careful not to be greedy [...]"[60]

Having given his orders and imposed his tyrannical prohibitions, Jesus did not stop there. In a dominating attitude, typical of aggressiveness, he sought to be obeyed at all costs. In this sense, he would spontaneously use different techniques. To begin with, he did not hesitate to indulge in blackmail, threatening the worst evils to anyone who violated his orders and multiple prohibitions. This is what we see when we read between the lines of the Gospels.

At first, he seemed to consider physical violence. They are indicative of a highly aggressive personality, and will not fail to generate real reprisals on occasion:

---

58. *Matthew* (19:17-19), see also *Matthew* (10:5-6), (17:9), *Luke* (9:55), (18:20), *John* (8:11).
59. *Luke* (12:4-5).
60. *Luke* (12:15), see also *Matthew* (5:34-37), (5:39-42), (6:7-8), (6:19), *Luke* (12:16-21).

"And his master was angry and delivered him to the executioners, until he had paid all that he owed. This is how my heavenly Father will treat you, unless each of you forgives his brother with all his heart."[61]

He did not only attack men:

"As Jesus was leaving the temple, his disciples came up to him to point out the buildings. But he said to them, 'Do you see all this? Truly I say to you, there will not be left here one stone upon another that will not be thrown down."[62]

And his aggressive threats could go up another notch:

"But woe to you Pharisees, for you tithe mint and rue and all herbs, and neglect justice and the love of God, which is what you should have done, not leaving out the other things. Woe to you, Pharisees!"[63]

Many times, Jesus was more definitive:

"...unless you repent, you will all perish equally."[64]

Even beyond death, Jesus was vindictive towards those who refused to accept his teaching:

"I tell you the truth, unless you are converted and become like little children, you will not enter the kingdom of heaven."[65]

Finally, as a climax to this sinister crescendo, Jesus threatened the recalcitrant with hell:

"At the end of the world] the Son of Man will send his angels, who will take out of his kingdom all the offenders and those who

---

61. *Matthew* (18:35), see also *Luke* (12:47).
62. *Matthew* (24:1-2).
63. *Luke* (11:42-43).
64. *Luke* (13:3, 5), see also *Matthew* (15:13-14), (18:6), (21:44-46), *Luke* (17:1-3).
65. *Matthew* (18:3), see also *Matthew* (5:20), (12:36-37), *Mark* (8:38), *Luke* (9:26).

commit iniquity, and they will throw them into the fiery furnace, where there will be weeping and gnashing of teeth."[66]

Aggression can take another, more subtle form, which consists in reinforcing one's ascendancy over others by making promises. This is a technique well known to politicians, who aim to gain more and more control over the masses. Promises, especially those that are impossible to fulfill, are the insidious counterpart of threats. The threat constitutes a promise of unpleasantness, which denotes an obvious aggressiveness. The positive promise, by mirror effect, is no less malicious, not only because of its bad intention (the control of the crowd), but also because of its perfidy (the aggressiveness is masked).

Promises are an extremely powerful political tool. The hope they give rise to when the present situation is unpleasant, makes it possible to endure these unpleasantnesses, for a long, long time, or even all one's life if this commitment concerns the hereafter. Jesus intuitively understood this principle, which is so popular with politicians: it is with hope that one leads the crowds.

The promise to which Jesus most often resorted is immense. He said that by obeying his commands, which were particularly demanding, the believer would obtain...

"Truly I say to you, there is no one who has left his house, or his brothers, or his sisters, or his mother, or his father, or his children, or his lands, for my sake and for the sake of the good news, who will not receive a hundredfold, now in this age, houses, brothers, sisters, mothers, children, and lands, with persecutions, and in the age to come, eternal life."[67]

However, if eternity wasn't enough, Jesus promised... everything!

---

66. *Matthew* (13:41-42), see also *Matthew* (11:20-24), (18:8-9), (23:33, 36), *Mark* (9:42-48), *Luke* (10:12-15), (13:27-28).
67. *Mark* (10:29-30), see also *Matthew* (5:3-5, 12), (19:29), *John* (6:35), (6:47), (8:51-52).

"Whatever you ask in my name, I will do, so that the Father may be glorified in the Son. If you ask anything in my name, I will do it."[68]

A thorny question arises: how could men believe in such excessive promises, when experience teaches daily how limited and mortal living beings are?

What better tools can the tyrant use to control the masses than threats or promises? Both at the same time, of course. It is the bargaining, which signs at the same time the insidious return of a trait of the anal character. It consists in declaring: if you do what I say, then I promise you wonders; if you don't, then I threaten you with misfortune. It is an apparent "give and take". The relationship with others becomes a commercial exchange, in which obedience is exchanged for... wind. "Deeds for words" may well be a sublimated form of greed.

Jesus thus declared:

"I tell you, whoever declares himself publicly for me, the Son of Man will also declare himself for him before the angels of God; but whoever denies me before men will be denied before the angels of God. And whoever speaks against the Son of Man, he shall be forgiven; but whoever blasphemes against the Holy Spirit, he shall not be forgiven."[69]

In the line of this indirect aggressiveness, it is logical to see a more obvious symptom appear. Jesus seems to have had recourse to insults[70]. This is rather unexpected for a representative of God, or even a wise man:

---

68. *John* (14:13-14), see also *Matthew* (7:7), *John* (15:7).
69. *Luke* (12:8-10), see also *Matthew* (10:32-33), (16:25), *Mark* (8:35), (16:16).
70. *Matthew* (7:5), (7:11), (7:26), (12:38-39), (16:4), (17:17), *Mark* (7:5-6), *Luke* (9:41), (11:13), (11:29), (11:39-40), (12:1), (12:56), (13:15)

CHAPTER III: THE PARANOIA OF JESUS

"As for me, I know him [God]; and if I said I did not know him, I would be like you, a liar."[71]

"Woe to you, blind drivers! [...] Fools and blind men! [...] Serpents, race of vipers!"[72]

"Woe to you, scribes and Pharisees, hypocrites! For you are like whitened sepulchres, appearing beautiful on the outside, you appear righteous to men, but inside you are full of hypocrisy and iniquity."[73]

"Races of vipers, how could you say good things, wicked as you are?"[74]

After driving the pigeon sellers out of the temple, he said, "It is written, 'My house shall be called a house of prayer,' but you make it a den of robbers. But ye make it a den of thieves."[75]

As the most prosaic experience teaches, insults often precede violence.

If Jesus does not embody the word of God, there is only his aggressiveness to explain why he allows himself violence, without the slightest self-defense:

"They came to Jerusalem, and Jesus entered the temple. He began to drive out those who were selling and buying in the temple; he overturned the tables of the moneychangers, and the seats of the pigeon sellers; and he did not let anyone carry anything through the temple."[76]

On the theme of aggressiveness, what a surprise to discover a Jesus with a grudge: did he not harbor blatant desires for revenge?

"Then he [Jesus in the kingdom of God] will say to those on his left [who did not follow him while he was alive]: Depart from

---

71. *John* (8:55).
72. *Matthew* (23: 16-17, 33).
73. *Matthew* (23:27-28).
74. *Matthew* (12:34).
75. *Matthew* (21:13), see also *Mark* (11:17) and *Luke* (19:46).
76. *Mark* (11:15-16), see also *Luke* (19:45-46) and *Matthew* (21:12).

me, you cursed; go into the eternal fire that has been prepared for the devil and his angels. For I was hungry, and you gave me no food; I was thirsty, and you gave me no drink; I was a stranger, and you took me in; I was naked, and you clothed me not; I was sick and in prison, and you visited me not."[77]

In particular and against all odds, Jesus seemed to keep a dog from his bitch to Judas:

"The Son of Man is going away, as it is written about him. But woe to the man through whom the Son of Man is delivered! It would be better for that man if he had not been born."[78]

That Jesus did not forgive Judas is curious. He was supposed to have foreseen this betrayal well in advance, and he enjoined forgiveness. This fact attracts the attention of the investigating psychologist...

All this aggressiveness of Jesus, in its multiple forms, could not fail to generate quarrels and disputes. The Gospels show that Jesus' life was full of such complications.

To begin with, Jesus seemed to be deliberately performing forbidden acts, hence the predictable wrath of the lawful.

"Therefore the Jews persecuted Jesus, because he did these things on the Sabbath day. But Jesus said to them, 'My Father has been doing this until now; I am doing it too. For this reason the Jews sought all the more to kill him, not only because he violated the Sabbath, but because he called God his own Father, making himself equal with God."[79]

According to the Gospels, his assertions and his attitude triggered violent reactions:

------

77. *Matthew* (25:41-43), see also *Matthew* (12:31), *Mark* (3:28-30), *Luke* (12:9-10).
78 *Matthew* (26:24), see also *Mark* (14:21), *Luke* (22:22).
79. *John* (5:16-18), see also *Luke* (6:11), (13:14), (14:3-4), *John* (10:33).

"[After Jesus told the Jews that he existed before Abraham, they were incensed] Thereupon they took up stones to throw at him; but Jesus hid himself, and went out of the temple."[80]

A fortiori, a threat of death uttered by Jesus augured serious complications to come:

"Whoever falls on this stone will be broken, and whoever it falls on will be crushed [end quote]. The chief priests and the scribes tried to lay hands on him that very hour, but they feared the people. They understood that it was for them that Jesus had told this parable."[81]

Finally, in reaction to his provocations, threats and other insults, Jesus' contemporaries became extremely aggressive towards him. They even went so far as to wish him dead, which indicates how much they had become irritated by him:

"[...] the chief priests, the scribes, and the leaders of the people sought to destroy him..."[82]

They found a way to destroy him by handing him over to the Romans, who crucified him - the predictable result of the hatred he had aroused by his aggressive attitude[83].

Not only does Jesus seem to have fallen out with many, but his promise of internecine warfare did not go unheeded:

"So there was a division among the crowd because of him."[84]

One value that comes from Christianity is the condemnation of denunciation, because Judas denounced Jesus to the Romans. Therefore, the following advice is paradoxical:

---

80. *John* (8:59), see also *John* (18:21-22).
81. *Luke* (20:18-19).
82. *Luke* (19:47), see also *Mark* (3:6), (11:18), (14:1), *Luke* (22:2).
83. *Matthew* (26:47-50), (27:1-2), (27:20), (27:22), (27:39, 44), *Mark* (15:11), (15:12-15), (15:18-20), (15:32), *Luke* (22:63-64).
84. *John* (7:43).

"If your brother has sinned [and] he will not listen to you, take one or two people with you, so that the whole matter may be settled on the statement of two or three witnesses. If he refuses to listen to them, tell the Church [...]"[85]

Aggression is very often accompanied by emotional coldness. Against all expectations, Jesus seemed to show indifference towards his own family, probably because they did not believe in him:

"Jesus' mother and brothers came to him, but they could not get to him because of the crowd. They said to him, 'Your mother and your brothers are outside, and they want to see you. But he answered, 'My mother and my brothers are those who hear the word of God and do it."[86]

After mentioning his aggressiveness in its many forms, let's look at other symptoms of Jesus.

He seemed to be in the grip of hallucinations. According to the Gospels, he often claimed to hear the voice of God, or even of Moses. His hallucinations were mainly auditory. The following case benefits from particularly favourable material conditions:

"After fasting forty days and forty nights, [Jesus] was hungry. The tempter came to him and said, 'If you are the Son of God, command these stones to become bread. [The devil] said to him, 'If you are the Son of God, throw yourself down [...]"[87]

Some hallucinations were also visual:

"As soon as Jesus was baptized [as an adult], he came up out of the water. And behold, the heavens were opened, and he saw the Spirit of God descending like a dove and coming upon him. And

---

85. *Matthew* (18:17).
86. *Luke* (8:19-21).
87. *Matthew* (4:2, 3 & 6), see also *Luke* (4:1-13).

behold, a voice came from heaven, saying, This is my beloved Son, in whom I am well pleased."[88]

A hallucination being by definition personal, its link with the success of Jesus appears at least obscure...

Here is a delusion that seems at first sight to be independent of the two previous groups of symptoms, namely aggression and hallucinations. Jesus seemed to have a strong sense of persecution. There are many passages that attest to this. Readers of the Bible will reply that he was indeed persecuted. This is partly true, although he himself caused most of his suffering. But more importantly, even if he did not directly cause his own persecution, a great mystery remains: If Jesus was a mere human, how could he have foreseen the bullying he was actually subjected to later?

"For Jesus knew from the beginning who the unbelievers were, and who was the one who would betray him."[89]

Jesus also had the constant feeling of being hated:

"But this happened so that the word written in the law might be fulfilled: They hated me without a cause."[90]

Jesus generalized the hatred and persecution he was about to suffer to the fate of his disciples:

"Blessed are you when men shall hate you, when they shall cast you out, and reproach you, and cast away your name as vile, for the Son of man's sake!"[91]

---

88. *Matthew* (3:16-17), see also *Mark* (1:9-11), *Luke* (1:21-22), *Matthew* (17:2-3 & 5), and *Luke* (10:18), (22:43-44).
89. *John* (6:64), see also *Matthew* (26:21), *Mark* (9:12), *Luke* (9:44), *John* (6:70-71), (18:4).
90. *John* (15:25), see also *John* (7:7), (15:24).
91. *Luke* (6:22), see also *Matthew* (5:11), (5:12), (10:17, 22-23), *Mark* (13:9, 13), *Luke* (21:12), (21:17), *John* (15:18), (15:20).

Although the evangelists most likely invented additional stories, alien to Jesus, they nevertheless respected the spirit of their master, giving their writings an atmosphere of persecution:

An angel of the Lord appeared to Joseph in a dream and said, "Arise, take the child and his mother, and flee to Egypt, and stay there until I speak to you; for Herod will seek the child to destroy him. [...] And when Herod was dead, behold, an angel of the Lord appeared to Joseph in a dream in Egypt, and said, Arise, take the young child and his mother, and go into the land of Israel; for they that sought the young child's life are dead."[92]

A feeling related to the delusion of persecution is the omnipresent suspicion. Very often Jesus seemed to enjoin suspicion, against false prophets, men, scribes, inner darkness, oneself, etc.[93]

"Take heed, watch and pray; for you do not know when that time will come. It will be like a man who leaves his house on a journey, hands over authority to his servants, tells each one his task, and orders the doorkeeper to watch. Watch therefore, for you do not know when the master of the house will come, whether in the evening, or in the middle of the night, or at the crowing of the cock, or in the morning; fear lest he find you asleep when he comes suddenly. What I say to you I say to all: Watch."[94]

As a result of this mistrust and sense of persecution, there is a definite inclination to concealment, secrecy, and even anonymity. According to the Gospels, Jesus often asked for discretion after a miraculous healing:

---

92. *Matthew* (2: 13, 19-20).
93. See *Matthew* (7:15), (10:16-17), *Mark* (4:24), (13:5), (13:9), (13:23), *Luke* (11:35), (17:3), (20:45-46).
94. *Mark* (13:33-37).

"He healed all the sick, and he sternly admonished them not to make him known [...]"[95]

This concealment of his success contrasts sharply with his efforts to have his precepts accepted. Such a paradox is found in the subject of his divine ancestry:

"Then he charged the disciples not to tell anyone that he was the Christ."[96]

Similar discretion was required after the vision of Elijah and Moses:

"As they came down from the mountain, Jesus charged them not to tell anyone what they had seen, until the Son of Man had risen from the dead."[97]

Jesus also seemed to be very discreet about the places he frequented:

"Jesus left there and went into the territory of Tyre and Sidon. He went into a house, not wanting anyone to know about him, but he could not remain hidden."[98]

Finally, he advised others what was valid for him, as he did for mistrust or persecution. This typical transposition mechanism deserves special attention.

"When you pray, go into your room, close your door, and pray to your Father who is in the secret place..."[99]

This penchant for distrust was reflected in his taste for mysteries, which could be profitably compared to his esoteric language:

"At that time Jesus answered and said, 'I praise you, Father, Lord of heaven and earth, that you have hidden these things

---

95. *Matthew* (12:15-16), see also *Matthew* (8:4), (9:30-31), *Mark* (1:44), (5:43), (7:36), *Luke* (5:14), (8:56).
96. *Matthew* (16:20), see also *Mark* (3:11-12), (8:30), *Luke* (9:21).
97. *Mark* (9:9), see also *Matthew* (17:9).
98. *Mark* (7:24), see also *Mark* (9:30), *John* (7:10-11).
99. *Matthew* (6:6), see also *Matthew* (6:3-4).

from the wise and understanding, and have revealed them to children."[100]

This mania for secrets had its counterpart in the delirium of observation. The gospels seem to reveal, indirectly, that Jesus felt himself to be constantly observed by his "heavenly" father. If this father existed, such an impression would simply follow from divine ubiquity. Knowing that this is not the case, here is another mystery to explain. Where did he get this impression of being constantly watched?

"There is nothing hidden that should not be discovered, nor anything secret that should not be known. Therefore, whatever you say in the darkness will be heard in the light, and whatever you say in the ear in the chambers will be proclaimed from the housetops."[101]

But once again, what Jesus was transposing to the outside world was especially true for him. This phenomenon deserves a serious explanation. Although he thought he was being observed, it was precisely he, Jesus, who showed this strong tendency to observe others. This is logical, given that he was himself suspicious and secretive. Some passages betray a very observant, even "psychologist" Jesus:

"The scribes saw Jesus forgive a paralytic and said to themselves, How can this man speak like that? How can this man speak like that? He blasphemes. Who can forgive sins but God alone? Immediately Jesus, having known by his spirit what they were thinking within themselves, said to them, Why do you have such thoughts in your hearts?"[102]

---

100. *Matthew* (11:25).
101. *Luke* (12:2-3), see also *Matthew* (6:4), (6:6), (6:18), *Mark* (4:22), *Luke* (8:17).
102. *Mark* (2:7-8), see also *Matthew* (12:24-25), *Mark* (12:15), *Luke* (5:22), (6:7-8), (9:46-47), (11:17).

CHAPTER III: THE PARANOIA OF JESUS

At the time, this real ability to read the thoughts of others seemed inexplicable, which could lead superstitious minds to believe in a supernatural gift...

Another symptom, typical of Jesus, goes unnoticed if his divine ancestry is presupposed. According to the Gospels, Jesus appeared to be thirsty for justice. This would be normal, if he had come to earth with a mission, to impose a new order willed by God. Only in this case can the order of the time be seen as unjust, whether it be that of the Romans or the Jews.

Once this assumption is set aside, Jesus' obsession with justice, as with truth, reappears for what it is: incredible. He was one of those people who feel obscurely attacked by the "system" or "society". They can't stand the state of things around them, and always feel wronged, robbed, in other words, victims of injustice. But from this simple clinical observation to its understanding, a big step remains to be taken.

"Blessed are those who hunger and thirst for righteousness, for they shall be filled!"[103]

"Seek first the kingdom and justice of God [...]"[104]

And the feeling of being misunderstood is very close to this feeling of injustice:

"And I, because I speak the truth, you do not believe me."[105]

This abundance of symptoms, linked to delusions of persecution, obscures the understanding of the Jesus case, and even more so its success. How could his conviction of being hated have contributed to the diffusion of his ideas to those close to him? On the contrary, this aspect of the feeling of persecution could at

---

103. *Matthew* (5:6).
104. *Matthew* (6:33), see also *Matthew* (5:10), (5:11), (7:23), (12:7), (21:31-32), (24:12), *Luke* (18:6-8), (20:20), *John* (7:23-24)
105. *John* (8:45), see also *John* (8:43).

best explain why he hid and isolated himself, which refers to an earlier problem.

Jesus seems to have developed another characteristic symptom. He had great energy, an extraordinary enthusiasm in his grandiose projects. The accepted term in psychiatry is "hypersthenia," which etymologically translates as "excessive strength". It was very evident in Jesus' incredible outpouring of activity in promoting his worldview:

"Jesus went about all Galilee, teaching in the synagogues, preaching the good news of the kingdom, and healing every disease and sickness among the people."[106]

The following words could cover the same meaning, as a true formula of hypersthenia, which ignores itself:

"Ask, and it shall be given you; seek, and you shall find; knock, and it shall be opened unto you. For everyone who asks receives, and he who seeks finds, and to him who knocks it will be opened."[107]

And Jesus found a way to multiply his effectiveness, by making others work for his interests:

"When Jesus had finished instructing his twelve disciples, he departed from there to teach and preach in the cities of the country."[108]

According to the Gospels, Jesus was also characterized by a lively spirit, which appeared at the age of at least twelve:

"After three days, [his parents] found him in the temple, sitting among the teachers, listening to them and asking them questions. All who heard him were struck by his understanding and his answers."[109]

---

106. *Matthew* (4:23), see also *Matthew* (9:35), (19:1), *Mark* (1:39).
107. *Luke* (11:9-10).
108. *Matthew* (11:1).
109. *Luke* (2: 46-47).

CHAPTER III: THE PARANOIA OF JESUS

Jesus seemed to delight in presenting an apparently logical thread to his long speeches. These semblances of reasoning, these "ratiocinations", were manifested in particular by the numerous "because", "because because", "therefore", etc., which peppered his curious mode of expression. These linking words gave an impression of systematic coherence, albeit based on delusions. To designate this abundance of discourse, and this sick propensity for empty and fastidious arguments, psychiatrists use the term *logorrhea*, which etymologically means "flow of ideas". Let us at least hope that Jesus understood himself, in the meanders of his sinuous reasoning:

"Every kingdom divided against itself is laid waste, and every city or house divided against itself cannot stand. If Satan casts out Satan, he is divided against himself; how then shall his kingdom stand? And if I cast out demons by Beelzebul, by whom do your sons cast them out? Therefore they themselves will be your judges. [Etc.]"[110]

Another subtle trait is apparent in the words of the Gospels. Jesus seemed lucid, especially about himself and about what those around him thought of him. He was clear-sighted in perceiving the resistance that his assertions met with, to say the least, disconcerting. Here are two illustrations, among the Jews and in his own family:

"I know that you are Abraham's seed; but you seek to kill me, because my word does not enter you."[111]

Jesus also felt that "... neither did his brothers believe in him."[112]

No man is a prophet in his own country[113].

---

110. *Matthew* (12:25-27).
111. *John* (8:37), see also *Mark* (8:31), *Luke* (17:25).
112. *John* (7:5).
113. See *Luke* (4:24).

At the convergence of the overinflated ego and aggression, a clear feeling of superiority inevitably arises. Aggression, by distilling hateful feelings towards others, leads to a belittling of others, while symmetrically the aggressive person considers himself to be higher. These two symptoms are so correlated that cause and effect are intimately intertwined: is it the swelling of one's ego that engenders the aggressive belittling of others, or the reverse? In short, the coexistence of an inflated ego with a feeling of superiority is hardly surprising. What is more surprising is that Jesus seems to have been primarily concerned by this symptom, especially in the form of pretension:

"[...] I am gentle and humble of heart."[114]

A bit of pedantry also embellished his smugness, Jesus implicitly finding himself rich in good advice:

"Instruct yourselves by a comparison drawn from the fig tree."[115]

This venerable instruction, awarded to oneself, was not without a certain intelligence in his eyes:

"He who can understand, let him understand."[116]

Jesus was also very precious to those closest to him:

"[...] you always have the poor with you, and you can do them good when you want, but you don't always have me."[117]

If we take off the Christian glasses and give Jesus the simple status of a man, we can see how amazing this feeling of superiority was:

"You are from below; I am from above."[118]

---

114. *Matthew* (11:29), see also *Matthew* (20:15).
115. *Mark* (13:28).
116. *Matthew* (19:12), see also *Matthew* (16:8-9).
117. *Mark* (14:7).
118. *John* (8:23), see also *Matthew* (17:17), *Mark* (6:32), *John* (10:11), (10:16), (13:15).

"Are you still without intelligence, and do you not understand?"[119]

This feeling of superiority was naturally accompanied by great self-confidence:

"On the Sabbath day Jesus entered the synagogue and taught. They were amazed at his teaching, for he taught as one having authority, and not as the scribes."[120]

The feeling of superiority has other facets, including a certain weakness for flattery:

He said to Simon, "Do you see this woman? I came into your house, and you gave me no water to wash my feet; but she wet them with her tears and wiped them with her hair. You did not give me a kiss, but she, since I entered, has not stopped kissing my feet. You did not pour oil on my head, but she poured perfume on my feet. Therefore, I tell you, her many sins were forgiven: for she loved much. [...] Jesus said to the woman, Your faith has saved you; go in peace."[121]

Jesus could still appear to be susceptible:

"[Ten lepers went away after receiving Jesus' care, but] One of them, seeing that he was cured, went back, glorifying God with a loud voice. He fell on his face at Jesus' feet and gave thanks. He was a Samaritan. Jesus answered, Were not the ten healed? And the other nine, where are they? Is there no one else but this stranger who returns and gives glory to God?"[122]

He was also capable, on occasion, of sulking after being offended, and of engaging in a kind of emotional blackmail:

---

119. *Mark* (8:17).
120. *Mark* (1: 21-22).
121. *Luke* (7:44-47, 50), see also *Matthew* (26:10), *Mark* (14:6).
122. *Luke* (17:15-18), see also *John* (8:48-49).

"Behold, your house shall be left unto you desolate; but I say unto you, that ye shall see me no more, until ye shall say, Blessed is he that cometh in the name of the Lord."[123]

Vanity represents another aspect of the feeling of superiority. It consists of a heightened sensitivity to the good opinion of others. Although he enjoined distrust of false prophets, Jesus seems to have been seduced by the prospect of increased prestige:

John said to him, "Teacher, we saw a man casting out demons in your name, and we stopped him because he did not follow us. Jesus answered, 'Do not stop him, for there is no one who performs a miracle in my name who can immediately speak evil of me. [...] And whoever gives you a cup of water to drink in my name, because you belong to Christ, truly I say to you, he will not lose his reward."[124]

Jesus seemed to manifest another symptom, sometimes concomitant with vanity: interest (as in the case of divine bargains, "paradise for obedience"). Jesus' calculating spirit is linked to his emotional coldness and his anal character. Here is an illustration:

"When you are invited by someone to a wedding, do not take the first place, lest among the guests there be someone more prominent than you, and the one who invited you both come and say to you, 'Give way to that person. Then you would be ashamed to take the last place. But when you are invited, go to the last place, so that when the one who invited you comes, he may say to you, 'My friend, go up higher. Then it will bring you honor in front of all those who are at the table with you."[125]

Jesus' sense of superiority found expression in another indirect way. Jesus seemed to show an attitude of extreme exigency

---

123. *Luke* (13:25), see also *Matthew* (23:39).
124. *Mark* (9:38-41), see also *Matthew* (15:32), *Luke* (8:37-39).
125. *Luke* (14:8-11).

CHAPTER III: THE PARANOIA OF JESUS

towards others, especially when it was in his own interest. In this respect, he proved to be a terrible person, who did not tolerate the slightest deviation from the rule:

"Be ye therefore perfect, even as your heavenly Father is perfect."[126]

With regard to the religious rules that already existed, Jesus constantly urged others to apply them strictly:

When he had prayed, he got up and came to the disciples, and found them sleeping with sadness, and said to them, "Why are you sleeping? Arise and pray, that ye enter not into temptation."[127]

However, with regard to these ancient rules, Jesus often demanded even more, in a surfeit of demands:

"But I say to you that everyone who looks at a woman to lust after her has already committed adultery with her in his heart."[128]

He also invented new rules of conduct, and insisted that they be followed:

"If your brother has sinned, rebuke him; and if he repents, forgive him. And if he has sinned against you seven times in one day, and seven times he comes back to you, saying, 'I repent,' you will forgive him: I repent, you shall forgive him."[129]

Finally, with regard to those who decided to follow him, he was still terribly difficult:

"Therefore, whoever of you does not renounce all that he has cannot be my disciple."[130]

This delusional hold on others, in the service of his all-powerful ego, could take the classic form of jealousy:

---

126. *Matthew* (5:48).
127. *Luke* (22:45-46), see also *Luke* (18:1).
128. *Matthew* (5:28), see also *Matthew* (5:21-22), (5:31-32).
129. *Luke* (17:3-4).
130. *Luke* (14:33), see also *Matthew* (10:38-39), *Mark* (8:34), *Luke* (9:23), (14:25-27).

"He who loves his father or mother more than me is not worthy of me, and he who loves his son or daughter more than me is not worthy of me [...]"[131]

How can we explain the concomitant presence of all these personality traits, so incompatible with the usual image of Jesus?

A small detour through psychological knowledge is required.

In the common opinion, paranoia corresponds to the delusion of persecution. If it is true that it is part of it, it is not the only one, and it is not necessarily present. In fact, all the symptoms mentioned above have to do with paranoia. Let us now try to understand how.

Paranoia is a psychosis. As such, it shares a fundamental mechanism with schizophrenia: the withdrawal from the world. Let us recall that this mechanism is broken down into two stages, with the reflux of impulses, followed by the reconstruction of an imaginary universe through delusions and hallucinations. This pathological mechanism leads to other consequences, which we will detail now, before specifying the specificity of paranoia.

By withdrawing his interest from reality, the young autistic person turns away from his parents, or the educators who take their place. This is very detrimental to the formation of his mind. To understand why, we must look at what happens in normal times.

The formation of the identity of a healthy child, the construction of his self, passes by the identification with his close relations, which are generally his parents. The very young boy identifies himself with his father, by playing with cars. The little girl plays with dolls, by identification with her mother. By integrating these adult figures in his mind, the child assimilates a kind of second self, quite normal, which Freud calls the "super-ego". The superego is simply a mental representative of the parents, inside

---

131. *Matthew* (10:37), see also *Luke* (14:25-27).

the mind of the young child. This one dialogues with himself, telling himself what he must do. It is a conversation between his ego and his super-ego.

This first formation of the superego, by identification with the "great ones" having authority, constitutes the crucible in which the rules orchestrating the relations between men - the moral as well as the legal laws - will later flow. In other words, this first formation is at the origin of a superego having integrated all these laws, and which is quite simply the moral conscience. It is a kind of inner voice, which manifests itself each time a choice has to be made, about the right course of action.

Believers, such as Rousseau and Kant, have attributed this inner voice to God. Rousseau speaks of this consciousness as a divine instinct, and Kant calls it a "categorical imperative", that is to say an unconditional order[132]. Freud, for his part, determined the psychological origin of this voice. It comes from the identification of children with the "big ones", in general the parents.

In the normal subject, the superego and the self are opposed. The superego does not cease to brandish laws and prohibitions each time the self plans to carry out a desire, resulting from the id. Its action is very effective. It also works directly against the id, by repressing the asocial desires, so that they cannot even go up to the consciousness of the self. To achieve this, the superego borrows its force from the aggressive impulses, which it turns against the self, in the form of feeling of guilt.

However, the first desires of the young child are naturally directed towards his close relations, starting with his parents. This is the famous Oedipus complex. The young boy would like to conquer the mother for him alone, and sees in his father a

---

132. See Rousseau (Jean-Jacques), *Émile ou De l'éducation*, chapter IV, and Kant (Emmanuel), *Critique of Practical Reason*.

rival. This first desire meets at once the hostility of the father, even of the society in general, which opposes a prohibition to its realization. It is the social prohibition of incest, at the base of the Oedipus complex. This prohibition obliges the small boy to be interested in other people or objects. This brake constitutes the first necessary step to sublimation, to divert positively the basic impulses towards socially valued interests.

Now that some important mechanisms of normal development have been recalled, we can return to the psychotic, to better understand his fundamental deviations. The young autistic person misses the first step of his entry into society. The very first contact with society is through the parents, or the child's first adult entourage. However, the little psychotic child loses interest in them, in order to concentrate his attention on himself. By doing so, he hardly identifies himself with his parents, and consequently does not form a solid superego which would come to oppose his overinflated self. A second step is missed: directing only few desires towards his entourage, the small psychotic desires little his mother, principle of the Oedipus complex. He does not have either to face the prohibition of the father, or of the society in general against incest. The young psychotic does not face the opposition of a constraining law, which he should integrate into his superego to reinforce it. This weak and not constraining superego does not capture enough the aggressive impulses to turn them against the self. The psychotic will hardly know the bad conscience.

Here is the first characteristic of the psychotic: an absence of opposition between ego and super-ego. To the point that, loving only himself, the psychotic can only be interested in the beings who resemble him the most. A very curious reversal occurs, fundamental in psychosis. The Oedipus complex is reversed.

The little boy does not hate his father as a rival, but loves him as a being identical to himself. Not only there will not exist opposition between ego and super-ego in the adult psychotic, but love will unite them. The Oedipus complex is then reversed. The superego of the psychotic, instead of aggressively criticizing the self, will act in opposite mode: it will show itself encouraging as well as loving. From then on, where will the natural aggressiveness of the psychotic go? It can only turn towards the outside, which reinforces the rejection of the external reality, the parents, the society, and in particular their laws. The psychotic rejects the external laws.

The figure of the adult psychotic starts to take shape: a being who likes himself, whose superego encourages the self, and who did not internalize the social laws. This superego works in reverse mode: instead of receiving the rules of the society and of making them respect by the self against the id, it rejects them and replaces them by personal laws, resulting from the unconscious impulses. Then it encourages the self to realize them!

Aggression turns outward. Blaming others is preferred to condemning oneself. A normal man learns to contain his aggressiveness in order to express benevolence towards those around him. On the contrary, the psychotic can express aggressiveness towards those around him.

It is the case if it is added to this informal psychosis the high dose of aggressiveness of the anal character. This very rare configuration generates a detonating cocktail. Two elements are superimposed on schizophrenia: on the one hand, a stubborn organization; on the other hand, a lot of aggressiveness, this time directed towards the world. This meeting generates the "systematized delirium", the other name of paranoia, in which aggressiveness predominates (with the feeling of superiority, tyranny, etc.).

We still have to detail the process of formation of a delusion, and then study the way in which it is systematized, i.e. logically developed and obstinately defended against all denials of reality.

The delusion is a false idea which results from a projection, that is to say an attribution to reality of an unconscious element. Erotomania is an example of delusion, in which the subject projects love of himself. It consists in believing oneself to be loved by someone. The unconscious "I love me" can become, in the consciousness of the delusional, "this woman loves me", for example. In other words, the love that the paranoid has for himself is projected onto someone else.

Projection is a very important psychological mechanism, especially in explaining paranoia. In everyday life, it is very common to attribute to others what is only true for oneself.

Sometimes, projection is the right way to perceive the unconscious of another person. A person who believes that he or she is being persecuted by someone may by chance come across someone who is really aggressive, even if this aggressiveness remains unconscious. In this case, projection allows one to perceive another reality, that of the unconscious of the other person.

The projection itself comes from the basic psychotic phenomenon, according to which the subject sees only the reflection of his unconscious through the window of reality.

Once his delusion is in place, the paranoid defends against all denials what he judges to be true, with the stubbornness of the anal character. He systematizes his delusion. In the case of erotomania, if the person supposedly in love denies it, the paranoid builds up endless explanations. He explains that he dares not declare his love out of modesty, or that he is acting in bad faith, or that he is not yet aware of it, etc. The paranoid can then become dangerous. His aggressiveness does not support this supposed dishonesty of his entourage, which refuses what the paranoid holds to be true.

After this detour through the knowledge of psychology, comes the moment of application to the Jesus case.

In a clinical reading of the Gospels, Jesus seemed particularly aggressive, as revealed by his warlike incitements, his orders, his prohibitions, his tyrannical game of threats and promises, his insults, his angry violence, his desire for revenge, his quarrels, his provocations, his incitement to denunciation, his high opinion of himself, his claim to divinity, and his emotional coldness.

Aggression does not require an explanation. It is a basic, irreducible impulse, common to all animals. What matters most to the psychologist is its future. Certainly, all men are aggressive, at least unconsciously. However, different solutions present themselves to channel this aggressiveness, which determines as many different personalities.

The ideal is to sublimate one's aggressiveness. It can then be expressed in a healthy way, for example in competitive emulation in scientific research, where each competitor tries to surpass himself to reach the best level of knowledge.

A part of the aggressiveness of the subject gains to return on itself, so that its superego represses from the interior the asocial impulses of the unconscious. It is the condition of their sublimation. Not to sublimate leads to the brutal expression of aggressiveness, in violence and destruction in particular. Jesus seemed not to have renounced these archaic ways of flowing.

Often, social rituals, especially politeness, are used to regulate aggression. But Jesus' overflow of gall drove him to deny the rules of courtesy, and even to seek to impose other rituals.

Finally, another way remains open, which is projection. Knowing that, in general, it consists in attributing to the external reality a property of the subject himself, a hallucination is simply a sensory projection on a concrete object, instead of being the projection of an idea or a feeling on others. Jesus was used to sensory projections. But he also projected his own personality traits. As a man of immense charisma, he was suspicious of such a characteristic in others:

"Beware that no one deceives you. For many shall come in my name, saying: I am he. And they shall deceive many."[133]

In a similar way, the vanity of Jesus was highlighted. In particular, he advised people to make calculations in order to be prominent in the assemblies[134]. Yet he suspected others of being conceited:

"Beware of the scribes, who love to walk about in long robes, and to be greeted in the public places; who seek the first seats in the synagogues, and the first places at feasts; who devour widows' houses, and make long prayers for the sake of appearance. They will be judged more severely."[135]

Jesus made projections that came up much more often than others - starting with the one at the heart of his delusion of persecution.

This one consists in the projection of aggressiveness, which is attributed to others. Such is the origin of the delusion of persecution. This mechanism allows the persecuted to supposedly justify the direct expression of his own hatred.

Let's elaborate a bit on this particular delusion, which is one of the three main paranoid delusions of Jesus.

As noted above, the New Testament reader will point out that Jesus was indeed persecuted, hated, betrayed, and eventually sentenced to death. He will deduce that Jesus was not paranoid.

---

133. *Mark* (13:5-6), see also *Matthew* (24:4), (24:11).
134. *Luke* (14:8-11).
135. *Mark* (38-40), see also *Matthew* (23:5, 14).

Furthermore, the believer will assert that Jesus anticipated his actual persecutions, which would indicate a visionary gift, proving his divinity:

Jesus took the twelve with him and said to them, "Behold, we are going up to Jerusalem, and all that has been written by the prophets about the Son of Man will be fulfilled. For he will be handed over to the Gentiles, and they will mock him, and insult him, and spit on him, and scourge him and kill him..."[136]

It is a beautiful system, perfectly coherent at first sight.

For the atheist, on the contrary, a mystery appears: how could Jesus have anticipated his real persecutions? To answer this question, we would like to have a clue. The structure of the Gospels undoubtedly contains a secret flaw.

But there is a thread that sticks out. We must grasp it, pull it out and follow it through the maze of Jesus' acts and their subsequent recounting by exalted believers.

Here is this crack, in the form of a surprising contradiction.

If Jesus had really predicted his fate with precision, if he had known in advance that he would be persecuted, betrayed, condemned to crucifixion, and then finally resurrected, would he not have submitted to this fate with calmness? He would have resigned himself calmly and wisely to fate, knowing in advance the path that would lead him back to his supposed father. Now a serious contradiction arises in the texts, which clearly state that Jesus was trying to escape his fate.

On one side is:

"Jesus, knowing all that was to happen to him [...]"[137]

But on the other hand:

---

136. *Luke* (18:31-33), see also *Mark* (9:31), (10:32-34), *Luke* (9:22).
137. *John* (18:4), see also *Matthew* (26:21), *Mark* (9:12), *Luke* (9:44), *John* (6:64), (6:70-71).

"Jesus went around Galilee, for he did not want to stay in Judea, because the Jews were trying to kill him."[138]

Why did Jesus try to escape from his executioners when he was supposed to know in advance his impending, inevitable end?

The contradiction lies between "precise knowledge of a written future" and "shameless flight from this known future". Changing one term in this contradiction, just one, is enough to resolve it and open up the mystery of Jesus' predictions. This is the *precise* term. In reality, Jesus did not have a precise knowledge of his future. He had a vague, intuitive knowledge of it, in fact a simple presentiment, which was not supernatural at all - but everything sickly. In this context, two questions arise: why did the evangelists write that Jesus knew his future precisely? And how could Jesus have any knowledge of his future?

To answer this second question, we must first ask ourselves another: why was Jesus really persecuted?

The study of his symptoms leaves no doubt on this point. The persecutions endured by Jesus are the direct consequence of his own aggressiveness. Chronologically speaking, Jesus was the first to harass others, with his admonitions, his orders, his threats, his contempt for religious customs and rules of propriety, his claim to be the only one to have the truth, his arrogance, his conviction of being the chosen one, his provocations, his violence, etc.

Here is one of many instances in which Jesus' aggressiveness leads to violence on the part of others: "[After inventing a parable in which a vineyard owner goes to kill the vinedressers who have slaughtered his son and his servants] Whoever falls on this stone will be crushed by it, and whoever it falls on will be crushed [the stone rejected by those who were building and which became the principal stone of the kingdom of God, promoted by Jesus].

---

138. *John* (7:1), see also *Matthew* (12:14-15), (2:22), *John* (11:53-54).

CHAPTER III: THE PARANOIA OF JESUS

When the chief priests and the Pharisees heard his parables, they understood that Jesus was talking about them, and they tried to seize him; but they feared the crowd, because they thought he was a prophet."[139]

If Jesus had been the son of God, he would have logically tried to impose new religious laws, even if aggressively. Without God, this aggressiveness is no longer justified. And in both cases, it is this aggressiveness that clearly triggered the harassment against Jesus.

The question of the real cause of these persecutions has been examined. The question now arises as to whether Jesus anticipated it, albeit vaguely but really.

Several answers exist, all of them complementary.

First, as a psychotic, Jesus projected his own aggression onto those around him, allowing him to complain about it long before he was actually oppressed. Because of his sense of persecution, Jesus did anticipate his coming troubles, but not in the precise way that the evangelists claimed. He only intuitively, confusedly, sensed them.

Secondly, we have seen that projection is sometimes right, when it allows us to perceive certain contents in the unconscious of others. A delusion is false in reference to reality, though sometimes true in relation to the unconscious of others. The persecutors of Jesus really nourished aggressiveness, at first unconscious, then conscious and active. He was able to feel it before it was expressed. His projection allows him to perceive the unconscious of others before it becomes conscious and even more effective. A paranoid person is always very sensitive to the aggressiveness that still exists only in the unconscious of others, by dint of observing them with distrust. In this way, Jesus was able to anticipate his future persecutions, albeit in a vague and intuitive way.

---

139. *Matthew* (21:44-46), see also *Matthew* (26:65-67).

Finally, a statistical effect intervenes, a perspective effect which makes it seem remarkable afterwards that a paranoid, nurturing the fear of being persecuted, ends up actually becoming one. Let us take the case of the lottery. One hundred percent of the winners of a lottery started by playing. Likewise, one hundred percent of the rare paranoid individuals who have actually been persecuted first developed a persecutory delusion. This is inevitable. This fear can still pass for a divine premonition, provided one focuses on one's own unique case. To claim that the lottery winner had a genius intuition would be equally erroneous. This one-time occurrence puts aside the overwhelming majority of false predictions. The overwhelming majority of those who played the lottery lost. Statistically, among those who gambled, as well as those who complained about persecution in advance, a winner sometimes occurs. Jesus won the jackpot because he was more aggressive than the other "persecuted".

Why did the evangelists specify Jesus' vague but real anticipations after they were realized?

First, a phenomenon of retrospective distortion comes into play. The words are transformed by adding to them more precise data, obtained after the events that actually took place.

Second, the evangelists had an interest in distorting Jesus' claims. Blinded by their admiration, they relied on his paranoid fears to turn them into rigorous predictions. However, this rewriting work was approximate. They forgot to erase the evidence of their falsification: Jesus had tried to escape his fate.

What does this mean? Once the event has passed, evangelists are at liberty to reinterpret the vague presentiments of a paranoid. He must have feared persecution and betrayal, he must have sensed it, if only as a consequence of his constant aggression. Once he was really persecuted and betrayed, the evangelists attributed to Jesus much more precise words than he actually uttered. Their interest was in extolling the virtues of their idol. They later granted him visionary gifts, with this kind of phrase:

"I tell you the truth, one of you will hand me over.[140]

A second mistake of the evangelists appears. Not only did they leave a contradiction behind their deed, but they also betrayed their master without their knowledge. It is precisely because they repeatedly write that Jesus knew he would be bullied long before he actually suffered it, that the modern reader can establish the existence of his delusion of persecution. This supposedly divinatory anticipation consisted in saying that he was mistreated long before he actually was, in other words, in believing that he was persecuted when he was not. The evangelists, in believing to praise his foresight, betrayed their master. This mechanism applies to all the pathological symptoms of which they had no knowledge, and which they mostly described as supernatural gifts. They could not hide all these clues, unable to predict the progress of 20th century psychology.

The other symptoms related to this persecution delusion become transparent. Distrust, concealment and secrecy are direct consequences of this sick conviction of being persecuted.

The sense of injustice and the feeling of being misunderstood are interesting. They point to the obvious discrepancy between the abnormally functioning personality of Jesus and the healthy personality of his skeptical contemporaries. Jesus was certainly not in danger of being understood, since he was expressing out loud the direct productions of his unconscious, whereas normal men try to repress their id in order to adapt to social laws. They make the effort to integrate the basic rules of communication, in other words the social conventions on language, which allow

---

140. *Matthew* (26:21), see also *Luke* (9:44), *John* (6:70-71).

them to understand each other. Jesus was daydreaming, and his dreams were incomprehensible.

The delusion of observation developed by Jesus can be explained by the mechanism of projection. Where does this curious idea that God sees everything come from? Paranoids like to observe themselves. This is a direct consequence of the relationship between their superego and their ego, which functions in reverse mode, i.e. positive. Looking at themselves gives them pleasure, because they flatter themselves instead of criticizing themselves. Moreover, the superego is located between the ego and the id. It communicates with the one and the other. It plunges its roots in the id, having a privileged access to it. It sees "everything" there. Jesus attributed to God and to the world what was valid only for the functioning of his unconscious. God would see everything, in the same way that the superego perceives everything inside the mind, namely the id and the ego. To put it another way, Jesus was constantly observing himself with pleasure, and he assumed by transposition that God also scans everything.

Lucidity represents another characteristic very close to this delusion of observation. This capacity to see oneself realistically is the result of three distinct mechanisms: first, let us recall that the psychotic observes himself continuously; then, he can see himself better than a healthy person, insofar as he does not criticize or censor himself; finally, precisely, the psychotic has not integrated the external social laws, including morality. Also, he is not ashamed to see in himself impulses which are nevertheless condemned by society. In short, the paranoid does not bother with conventions to call a spade a spade, even if he would contravene the decorum of his environment. Conversely, this lucidity can be applied to others, all the better because his tendency to projections sometimes allows him to perceive their unconscious directly. Such was Jesus' supposed gift of observation, motivated at first by mistrust and a feeling of persecution.

The hypersthenia of Jesus, in other words the immense energy that he deployed for his cause, is also explained by the absence of opposition between his ego and his superego, typical of psychosis. Any normal man, before acting, is at least restrained by doubts, precautions, self-criticisms, scruples, the fear of doing badly, the fear of the glance of the others, the concern of the respect of the social rules, etc. It is the normal action of the ego and the superego. This is the normal action of the superego, which supervises and censors the possible outbursts of the impulses coming from the id. On the contrary, Jesus' superego encouraged him. His aggressiveness was never turned against himself, but always towards possible external obstacles, which made his action even more effective. This personality trait also provides a first element to explain one of the conditions of Jesus' success. Convincing the crowd of the interest of his ideas requires immense energy, *especially* when they are so delirious.

From this hypersthenia, added to the anal character, comes the possibility of acquiring an above-average intelligence. Studies require a good dose of willpower, and Jesus undoubtedly studied effectively. Secondly, having a clear mind is a benefit attributable, in good part, to the need for order, resulting from the anal character. Supplemented by a good faculty of sublimation, here is Jesus able to speak about abstract ideas with a certain ease. However, these mechanisms are not enough to explain his capacity to create new ideas, and especially ideas likely to fascinate the greatest number.

Jesus wanted everyone to love and obey him. In doing so, he betrayed a double characteristic of his unconscious mechanisms: his psychotic love for himself, and his anal character which implies taking pleasure in controlling men and events. Now, by adding the mechanism of projection, jealousy appears. Jesus attributed to others an egocentric interest in themselves, which hindered the love that he unconsciously wished to bring back upon himself. When he detected selfishness in others, the process remained the same. A simple projection of his personality led him to discover in others many "defects" that he wanted to correct, for the reason that he, Jesus, felt aggrieved by these defects of his loved ones. He sensed a self-love in others that made him lose control over them. He then demanded the love of God above all else, which was the same as loving him, Jesus, who identified himself with God. Turning them away from their ego brought them back to him.

Jesus' feeling of superiority had a double origin in his aggressiveness and his inflated ego. The latter was the result of a positive superego, hence this ascendancy over others, this conquering confidence.

As for Jesus' aggressiveness, it was such that it was expressed in every possible way: it generated the reactionary forms of the anal character, such as the concern for order (as long as this order was his); it was also directed towards other individuals, with its tyrannical precepts; it was also partly sublimated, to create aggressive parables. It sometimes exploded directly, with insults, provocations and violence. This feeling of superiority was expressed through the personality traits of a Jesus who was pretentious, touchy, resentful, vain, extremely demanding of others, prone to sulking, easy to flatter... This is not the common image of Jesus. But the psychological study of his case allows us to get singularly close to the real character.

His self-confidence was based on an inflated ego and an inverted Oedipus complex. He rejected the opinions of others and comforted himself in his own certainties by means of an inverted superego. The certainty of being right, seen with the anal character, also finds here a complementary explanation.

The paranoiac goes to look for "truths" in his own unconscious, without the barrier of the superego. He draws directly from it blinding convictions, which the general opinion does not manage to rectify. He draws from it deep convictions which, although in glaring gap with the commonly admitted truth, are not less defended with the obstinacy and the "systematism" proper to the anal character. Like hypersthenia, these traits help us understand how Jesus was able to impose his bizarre ideas on the crowd. He did not doubt himself and never hesitated. He made a strong impression on his listeners, who certainly did not have as much confidence in their own view of the truth.

His calculating spirit was also a direct result of his anal nature. It also contributed to his success, by making his action on those around him more effective.

Jesus had another interesting characteristic, which helps us to understand his ambiguous relationship with the crowds. In healthy people, the two main impulses, of life and death (love and hate), are split in two. Society teaches the subject to direct his positive impulses towards others, and to sublimate the negative ones (or to turn them partly towards himself to reinforce the superego). But Jesus did not know this internal conflict, between the destructive impulses of the id and the aggressive censorship of the superego. On the contrary, his two impulses turned outwards, without the slightest censorship: he loved those who followed him, while governing them aggressively. Of course, a good part of his hostility was directed towards those who stood in his way, those who did not believe in him. He was no less tyrannical towards those who followed him, while at the same time loving them. This curious phenomenon seems contradictory for the conscience. From the point of view of the unconscious of convinced listeners, this double movement is naturally felt as a paternal attitude: Jesus scolded his disciples while loving them, with the claim to protect them. In doing so, he almost involuntarily assumed the position of a father. A father must be both severe and benevolent. At the same time, Jesus was infantilizing the crowds.

Concerning the parables, a corner of the veil is lifted, thanks to the understanding of the mechanisms of paranoia. Jesus built his parables by projecting unconscious material onto the real world. He began with simple allusions to his unconscious, and then structured and defended them, based on his sense of organization proper to the anal character. The parables drew a vast system, a delusional system, which characterizes the paranoia.

The investigation is progressing. Many of Jesus' traits, from his schizophrenia to his anal retentiveness, have been clarified. His paranoia was the result of a meeting of the two. It consisted in reconstructing a universe from delusions, which were then organized between them. His delusions had for origin projections of his unconscious on the reality. To close this skein of mechanisms, Jesus tried to impose this imaginary world on the crowds with vigor and aggressiveness.

However, many questions remain.

Jesus' allusions to his own unconscious, brought to light by projection, concerned only himself. How could he interest others than himself with allusions to his personal id, even if they were constructed in a vast logical system? Why did his personal delusions fascinate the crowds? Why did his speech have an almost universal scope?

Moreover, a new conundrum arose in the meantime, insofar as these paranoid symptoms represented the exact opposite of the values he held. His effective resentment contradicted his demand for forgiveness. His warlike aggressiveness disproved the pacifist image of the wise man advocating love. His calculating spirit invalidated the ideal of selflessness, etc. How could he appear to believers, and even to atheists, as the exact opposite of what he was? And how could such an aggressive being inspire the love of the masses?

Chapter IV:
The Megaparanoia of Jesus

From what the Gospels suggest, Jesus' words seemed to be imbued with ideas of greatness, which took various forms.

To begin with, Jesus probably had a strong ambition:

"And I tell you that you are Peter, and on this rock I will build my church, and the gates of Hades shall not prevail against it.[141]

His success on this particular issue does not mean that his greed was healthy. The part of Jesus' ambition that succeeded was only a residue of infinitely larger and perfectly inadequate projects. When a person has a thousand plans, one of them may well come to pass. It is the tree that hides the forest.

Jesus probably developed another secondary symptom, close to ambition. It was his competitive spirit:

"I have a greater testimony than John [the prophet] [...]"[142]

Secondly, Jesus seemed to manifest many ideas of greatness, which can only be identified as such if one rejects his status as a prophet:

---

141. *Matthew* (16:18), see also *Mark* (16:15).
142. *John* (5:36).

He said to them, "Why did you seek me? Didn't you know that I have to take care of my Father's business? But they did not understand what he was saying to them."[143]

Megalomaniacs always think big, by definition. They usually address the cosmos directly, as if it were an interlocutor with whom they were dealing as equals, or even, in the case of Jesus, with a sense of superiority:

"You will have tribulation in the world; but take heart, I have overcome the world."[144]

The following passage reaches such a degree of delirium in grandeur that it is probably to be attributed to some inflamed evangelist. The latter, however, respects the state of mind of his master:

"Immediately after those days of trouble, the sun will be darkened, the moon will not give its light, the stars will fall from heaven, and the powers of the heavens will be shaken. Then the sign of the Son of Man will appear in heaven, and all the tribes of the earth will mourn, and they will see the Son of Man coming on the clouds of heaven with power and great glory. And he will send forth his angels with a great sounding trumpet, and they will gather his elect from the four winds, from one end of heaven to the other."[145]

Finally, even on a metaphorical basis, a nice hint of megalomania is clearly visible in the following famous passage:

"I am the light of the world; he who follows me shall not walk in darkness, but shall have the light of life."[146]

---

143. *Luke* (2: 49-50).
144 *John* (16:33).
145. *Matthew* (24:29-31), see also *Matthew* (12:6), (26:13), (26:53), (28:18-20), *Mark* (13:10), (16:15), *Luke* (21:25-27), *John* (9:5).
146. *John* (8:12).

Jesus' megalomaniacal relationship to reality was tinged with a particular coloring. If the Gospels are to be believed, Jesus had it in his head that the world was lost, or at least that it would be lost without his indispensable intervention, in extremis. This idea is not surprising in the corridors of psychiatric hospitals. The origin of such delusional thoughts remains a mystery, especially when they are supported by the credulous:

"[Many Samaritans are willing to believe Jesus] we know that he is truly the Savior of the world."[147]

Another classic delusion, among the many possible variations of megalomania, is the belief in immortality. Even though belief in an afterlife was common in his time, Jesus strangely overdid it with an existence before birth! More than a reincarnation, he envisaged a kind of divine eternity, a "prenatal immortality".

Jesus said to them, "Truly, truly, I say to you, before Abraham was, I am."[148]

And if many people believed in an immortal soul, on the other hand, few were those who thought they were prophets, messiahs, or *a fortiori* sons of God. Moreover, the tendency to make everything about oneself, which was revealed with schizophrenia, is found here, insofar as Jesus thought that the predictions of the Bible pointed to him personally.

"Speaking of himself while haranguing the crowd that had gone to see him in the desert] What did you go to see? A prophet? Yes, I tell you, and more than a prophet. It is he of whom it is written:

Behold, I send my messenger before your face,
To prepare your way before you."[149]

---

147. *John* (4:42), see also *Matthew* (18:11), (20:28), *John* (15:5).
148. *John* (8:58), see also *Matthew* (19:29), (26:32).
149. *Luke* (7:26-27), see also *Matthew* (2:5-6), (11:3-5), (26:54-56), *Luke* (4:43).

This intimate conviction of being a prophet seemed to be followed by a logical consequence, which is classic among all paranoids persuaded of being at the origin of a brilliant invention. It is the delusion of plagiarism, in other words the delusional conviction of being imitated. Jesus already feared that others would seduce the crowds. Here the same suspicion is raised a notch:

"If anyone then says to you: Christ is here, or, He is there, do not believe him. For false Christs and false prophets will arise."[150]

Now we come to one of the most important delusions of Jesus. His messianic delusion was always accompanied by the "delusion of filiation", which is recounted in many passages of the Gospels. Believing himself to be the son of God was a very interesting and fundamental singularity of Jesus. "I am not alone, but the Father who sent me is with me."[151]

This delusion of filiation was particularly complex, elaborate, or to put it in psychiatric terms, "systematized".

From the point of view of a modern atheist, Jesus' claims of divine ancestry appear simply for what they are: false. Clinging to an erroneous idea over a long period of time, despite all denials, is exactly what psychiatrists call a "delusion. In childhood, most men have doubted, at one time or another, that their official parents were their parents. This infantile thought largely persisted during the life of Jesus.

Why did he never stop claiming to be the "son of God"? Even if it were a metaphor, as some current atheists claim, who see Jesus as a wise man, the question remains: metaphor for what? The question is all the more pressing because this delusion of filiation was at the heart of all Jesus' conceptions. This central conviction had taken many different, even contradictory, forms in his words.

---

150. *Matthew* (24:23-24), see also *Matthew* (24:5), *Mark* (13:21-22), *Luke* (21:8).
151. *John* (8:16).

First, of course, Jesus affirmed his divine kinship:
The high priest asked him again, "Are you the Christ, the Son of the blessed God? Jesus answered, 'I am. And you shall see the Son of man sitting at the right hand of the power of God, and coming on the clouds of heaven."[152]

Sometimes this delusion went further, to the point of identity fusion with God:

"He who has seen me has seen the Father; how do you say, 'Show us the Father'? Do you not believe that I am in the Father and that the Father is in me? The words that I speak to you I do not speak of myself; and the Father who dwells in me, he does the works. Believe me I am in the Father, and the Father is in me; if not believe at least because of these works."[153]

But another delusion of filiation appears very clearly, when Jesus declared himself "Son of Man" seventy-eight times in the Gospels[154]. This was certainly not an invention on his part (Ezekiel did the same). It was meant to refer to human beings in general. What does it mean to be a human being in general? Or even more simply, what need could Jesus have had to keep repeating that he belonged to the human race? It was a curious way of referring to man in general, which deserves a little investigation. And an additional contradiction appears with the divine filiation: son of God, or of man in general? Not to mention the classic question: what does it mean to consider oneself human and divine at the same time? In religious terms: was he human or divine? This old debate on the double nature, going back at least to the first schism of the Church with Nestorius, requires a new look, a psychological one.

---

152. *Mark* (14:61-62), see also *Matthew* (7:21), (11:27), (16:17), *Luke* (10:22), (22:70), *John* (5:19-20), (16:27).
153. *John* (14:9-11), see also *John* (16:15).
154. See especially *Matthew* (8:20), (24:30), *Mark* (14:62), *John* (5:27).

Finally, other delusions of filiation have appeared concerning Jesus, although they were most certainly added after the fact by unscrupulous commentators. Unscrupulous, certainly; nevertheless, in inventing other fanciful filiations to Jesus, they at least respected the spirit of their idol, as far as the question of a simple, all-too-human kinship was concerned.

These late delusions consisted of ridiculous genealogies tracing him back from generation to generation to Abraham[155] or even God[156]. Another idea, original to say the least, has had a wide following: the mother of Jesus would have remained a virgin[157]. This delusion has the merit of being the logical consequence of Jesus' own assertions, resolving his contradiction of a simultaneously human and divine filiation...

As a conclusion to these delusions of filiation, let us note the revealing common sense of some of Jesus' contemporaries: "The Jews murmured about him, because he had said, 'I am the bread that came down from heaven. And they said, 'Is not this Jesus, the son of Joseph, whose father and mother we know? How then does he say: I came down from heaven?"[158]

How did Jesus manage to convince the crowds of his divine ancestry, even though they might otherwise have believed in God and the prophets? The mystery remains. On *the other hand*, his images of "bread from heaven" and "divine filiation" have the merit of striking the minds, as the passage quoted above indicates...

At the time, the novelty of Jesus' ravings was surprising. Today, we are so used to them that it is difficult to see them as they are.

---

155. *Matthew* (1:1-17).
156. *Luke* (3:24-38).
157. *Matthew* (1:18), (1:25).
158. *John* (6: 41-42).

Friedrich Nietzsche devoted a good part of his life to hunting down the unnoticed consequences of Christianity. He opens our eyes to the following words:

"In Christianity, neither morality nor religion has any point of contact with reality. There are only imaginary *causes* ("God", "soul", "self", "free will", - or even "serf will"); only imaginary *effects* ("sin", "redemption", "grace", "atonement", "remission of sins"); only a trade between imaginary *beings* ("God", "spirits", "souls"); only an imaginary science of *nature* (anthropocentric; total absence of the notion of natural cause); an imaginary *psychology* made of a total misunderstanding of oneself, of hazardous interpretations of pleasant and unpleasant sensations, for example of the states of the *nervus sympathicus*, with the help of the symbolic language proper to religious and moral idiosyncrasy ("contrition", "remorse of conscience", "temptation of the Evil One", "nearness of God"); an imaginary *teleology* (the "kingdom of God", the "last judgement", the "eternal life") This world of pure *fiction* is distinguished - to its disadvantage - from the world of dreams, by the fact that the latter *reflects* reality, while the former falsifies, devalues and denies reality."[159]

The folly of grandeur and the delusion of filiation, proper to Jesus, were accompanied by very particular projections, which the Gospels have recorded without their knowledge. They consist in the creation of imaginary beings, which are attributed to reality, to explain or interpret it. Jesus invented myths, insidiously introducing a number of imaginary entities. The mystery lies in their origin. In the case of Jesus, how did he manage to invent them? In a world without God, we must explain not only where this

---

159 Nietzsche (Friedrich), "L'Antéchrist", in *Œuvres philosophiques complètes, op. cit.* vol. VIII, § 15, p. 172.

idea of God comes from, but also all the supernatural elements that are supposed to accompany it.

Jesus began by taking from the Jewish tradition at least the following elements: "God" (with his voice ringing in his ears), the "kingdom of God" (the "paradise"), the "law of God," the "justice of God" (as conformity to God's will and norms), the "truth of God" (which is supposed to be expressed through Jesus' mouth), mystery" (truth from God, partially inaccessible to man because of human limitation), "God's omniscience", "God's grace", "election" (as predestination or fate), "good" and "evil", the distinction between "soul" and "body" (flesh), "Satan" (the adversary, the "devil"), "spirits" and "demons" (who haunt the "possessed"), "angels", "sin" (the fault as disobedience to God), "blasphemy", "eternal punishment" (eternal punishment, divine punishment), "final judgment", heart", "purity", "happiness" (the blessed), "spirit" (which dwells in the heart of the believer), "atonement", "freedom" (the possibility of man to choose on the basis of true knowledge), "inspiration", "prophet", "messiah", etc.

Second, Jesus seems to have generously enriched this tradition with a few entities of his own, or at least given them new meaning: "repentance" (which precedes forgiveness), "forgiveness" (the redemption of faults and "redemption"), "saving from sins," "sanctification" (a "saint" being pure and separate), "peace" (between God and man through the blood of the cross), "social reversal" (the first shall be last, and vice versa), "resurrection" (insofar as it would be he and not his commentators who would have invented this fable), "eternal life" (for those whose faults are redeemed), being the "son of God", being the "light of the world", or even being "heavenly food", etc.

A series of questions then opens up: how could Jesus have invented all these illusory entities? How could he combine them with the entities imagined before him, to create an apparently coherent universe? And how could he convince the crowds of the real existence of this ghostly cosmos? We still lack elements to answer these questions.

Another aspect of the case of Jesus draws particular attention, namely his very curious relationship to the laws that preexisted him. In a singular way, Jesus often behaved immorally, or even irreligiously, in the sense that he did not respect the rules in force in his environment[160].

Let's look at some religious examples:

"Some of the Pharisees asked him: Why do you do what is not allowed on the Sabbath? Jesus answered them, [...] The Son of Man is master even of the Sabbath."[161]

Let us also remember that, according to the Gospels, he prevented an adulterous woman from undergoing her religious punishment, and that he overturned tables and seats in a temple[162].

More radically, Jesus appeared as a kind of rebel, a religious revolutionary, who claimed to oust any order that did not come from him. The following promise was especially valid for a hypothetical elsewhere:

"For whoever exalts himself will be humbled, and whoever humbles himself will be exalted."[163]

Jesus was not content to disobey the laws of his time, whether moral or religious. Like the paranoiacs, he went further by questioning these accepted rules. He invented new laws, new instructions, which he tried to make everyone respect:

---

160. See for example *Luke* (11:37-38), *John* (4:7-9).
161. *Luke* (6:2, 3 & 5), see also *Matthew* (12:10-13), *Mark* (2:27-28), *John* (5:10-13).
162. *Matthew* (21:12).
163. *Luke* (14:11).

"You have heard that it was said, 'An eye for an eye and a tooth for a tooth. But I say to you, do not resist the wicked."[164]

Likewise, Jesus changed the law of Moses on divorce by forbidding the breaking of what God had joined[165].

This symptomatic relationship to the laws raises new questions: how could Jesus demand obedience when he himself so readily dispensed with it? And if God does not exist, where could he get his new laws from?

After these astonishing symptoms, the time has come to look for explanations to all these pathological manifestations, and answers to all these questions. To do this, a new detour through psychological knowledge is necessary.

Jung, a disciple of Freud, explored a deeper unconscious than the personal unconscious. This unconscious contains our own desires and memories, in short, everything that has made up the particularity of our individual path. In his work, Jung realized that a part of the unconscious of each man is different. It contains elements that are not specific to him, but belong to all the individuals of a society, even to humanity. He called it the "collective unconscious". These elements are very general symbols, which invariably have the same meaning, sometimes in all civilizations. He called them "archetypes". A simple illustration is the wind, which always refers to the spirit. In the Bible we find the "breath of God", and in the primeval forest a gust of wind can signal the passage of spirits.

Freud, for his part, discovered that certain projections are very particular. In the same way that archetypes are symbols common to a group of humans, certain projections attribute to reality forms from the collective unconscious. More exactly, these

---

164. *Matthew* (5:38-39).
165. *Mark* (10:2-9).

particular projections attribute to reality entire structures of the unconscious, instead of this or that personal content. But these structures remain the same for all men, like the ego, the id and the superego.

They are a special kind of projections that feed on elements common to social groups (the archetypes), or structures of the unconscious that are identical for all men. Insofar as the result of these projections is a myth, Freud calls them "mythical projections".

What is a myth? It is a fictional story that involves symbolic characters, and that allows to explain the origin of a real fact or object. The myth of Narcissus is instructive. This character admired his own image in the water of a river. A god punished him mortally for this, and turned him into a flower. This story is supposed to explain the origin of narcissus.

To understand the way in which a myth is produced from a projection of the structure of the unconscious, a well-known illustration will suffice. The myth of Oedipus tells the story of this unhappy hero, who was led to kill his father and make love to his mother. He had acted in spite of himself, without knowing who he was dealing with. In doing so, he was fulfilling desires that belong to the unconscious of all men: the Oedipus complex. Every child desires certain people around him and sees in others rivals, whom he would like to eliminate. It is a structure between three unconscious elements which is projected: the self, the father, the mother. They are connected by the two fundamental impulses: hate and love.

Oedipus is a fictional character. To believe in his existence would be to put on the account of reality a purely unconscious structure of desires.

Now, there had to be inventors of these myths, men showing a quite particular imagination, of a pathological nature. How did they do it, on the psychological level?

These particular men have access to the structures of their collective unconscious, which allows them to imagine myths, by delusion and projection. Some men are not satisfied with projecting the contents of their own unconscious, as simple paranoiacs do. These individuals, very rare, think big, and project either the archetypes, or the structures of unconscious common to all men.

These paranoids are megalomaniacs. They make mythical projections. They are "megaparanoids".

Jesus was a megaparanoid.

One of the greatest that the earth has ever borne.

At least one of those who was able to convince the largest number of men.

The megaparanoid projects the collective structures of his unconscious, as well as archetypes. These mythical projections can also be called "megaprojections". The megaparanoid wrongly attributes to the collective forms a reality of a special kind, which Freud calls "suprareality"[166]. This reality is not perceived, although it is supposed to explain the visible reality, the true one. God cannot be seen, but he is supposed to explain the origin of all that is perceptible, with Genesis. Freud discovered the real origin of this supra-reality, in this particular process that is the mythic projection. This is why he calls the productions that emanate from it "illusions"[167].

Let's linger a bit on this megaprojection, the biggest of the megaprojections: God. All men, having been children, include

---

166. See FREUD (Sigmund), *Psychopathology of Daily Life*, Paris, Payot, 1990, chapter XII, p. 296.

167. See FREUD (Sigmund), "The Future of an Illusion", in *Complete Works. Psychoanalysis*, Paris, PUF, 1994, volume XVIII, p. 172.

in their unconscious the model of the "great". Most often they are parents, or tutors, or educators in general. Insofar as no child can survive without the support of a grown-up, the existence of the whole society depends on the capacity of adults to fulfill this function. The primary function of these adults is to help. They protect and bring life and the will to live, which is an essential component of love.

The child thus integrates in him, in his deep unconscious, an ideal image, of a great one, which brings him love, help, protection.

This large one also assumes other essential functions, apparently in contradiction with the first ones. The little man needs a long education. The big ones will have to rectify the behavior of the child. This constraining part includes punishments, tantrums, etc. The grown-ups apparently show the opposite of love and protection. But it is for the child's own long-term good in his or her own adult life to come. The grown-up instills in the child the constraints that will be the constraints of reality, whether it be nature or society.

In the superego of the child the image of a great, severe but good, which brings constraints and laws to him is formed. It is the ideal of the self.

With the functions of the great, on one side the protection, the love, the taste of living, on the other side the constraints and the laws, an archetype appears. The ideal of the self. Its existence is purely psychic. It is only at the price of a megaprojection of this archetype, that can be attributed to him any reality, an illusory supra-reality.

These functions of the great, as an archetype of the collective unconscious, humanity has become aware of them as it goes along, mistakenly attributing them to reality. There are still some very precise ones that have not yet been brought to light at this or that time. This was the case of forgiveness. When a child makes mistakes in his learning of reality, the adult who educates him is obliged to scold him. Then, he must also "forgive" him, as mistakes are inevitable and part of learning. This moment of forgiveness gives the child immense pleasure; it is the moment of consolation after the anger, when the grown-up reminds him of his love and protection.

We can now apply these general mechanisms of the unconscious to delusions, mythical projections, symptoms and finally to the parables of Jesus.

Ideas of grandeur are directly derived from megaprojections from the collective unconscious. In some African tribes, when a person has a "dream from above," one of those important dreams that seem to carry an explanatory force about the mysteries of the universe, that person gathers the village together to tell the dream. This is the same process that is at play with Jesus' megalomania. Jesus was a daydreamer, although his kind of dreaming was very specific. He hallucinated the archetypes or structures of the collective unconscious. He felt their singular force, from which also resulted his deep conviction of holding the truth, alone against all. He did hold a truth, even a universal one, but not a truth that would concern reality, contrary to what he believed. In fact, he only held a truth about the unconscious, the collective unconscious more precisely. His metaphysical statements simply alluded to his unconscious, without his knowledge. Freud, having discovered this mechanism, opens the opposite way. This return to reality consists in re-translating, in the psychology of the unconscious, the myths relating to paradise and original sin, to God, to evil and good, to immortality, etc.[168]

---

168. See FREUD (Sigmund), *Psychopathology of Everyday Life, op. cit.* Volume XII, p. 296.

One of the ideas of greatness developed by Jesus is interesting, which consists in believing that he could save the world. More exactly, he intended to save it by giving his life. The general idea of "saving the world" is to be understood as a psychotic reconstruction of the world. Freud analyzed the writings of a great psychotic, Daniel-Paul Schreber. From the depths of his psychiatric hospital, this former president of a court of appeal claimed that he had to save the world by having himself impregnated by God[169]. He was much less successful than Jesus, the psychiatrists of the twentieth century being less credulous than the listeners of the first century, although the principle of his delusion was quite similar. He claimed that the cosmos was threatened with destruction, and that he had to rebuild it, to save it. This movement, already examined, is typically a psychotic one. The schizophrenic, after having withdrawn his impulses from the reality to bring them back on him, tries then to rebuild the universe from his unconscious. To do this, he makes abundant use of delusions, hallucinations and other projections. As for the curious motive of the fertilization by God, an unconscious homosexual component appears clearly there. This element comes from the oedipal inversion, in direct contact with the divine filiation professed by Jesus. To save the world, each one has his own method. Schreber confused his ego with the world, and asked for the fertilization of the unconscious father. Jesus' method was no less delirious, with his system of filiation. In short, two movements can be seen, typically psychotic: first, the psychotic withdraws his interest from the world, "therefore" the world is destroyed, then he becomes interested again, and "therefore" the world is

169. See FREUD (Sigmund), "Psychoanalytical remarks on a case of paranoia (*Dementia paranoides*) described in autobiographical form", ("The Schreber case", written in 1910, published in 1911), in *Complete works. Psychoanalysis, op. cit.* Volume X, pp. 225-304.

CHAPTER IV: THE MEGAPARANOIA OF JESUS

recreated. It is saved. To recreate the world after losing it is to save it. Moreover, Jesus was reinvesting the world on his own model of innocence, stemming from the positive relationship between self and superego. He "thus" recreated a world identical to himself, "without fault". This delusion of grandeur concludes "logically" with the certainty of "saving the world from its sins"!

The delusion of immortality is a classic. But Jesus, in a megalomaniacal overkill, added a prenatal immortality to it. He attained, in delusion, a sensation of eternity that is quite interesting on the psychological level. One of the most fundamental characteristics of the unconscious consists in ignoring time. Once an image, an act or a desire is perceived or lived, they are registered in the unconscious. They remain there forever, and continue to act there throughout the subject's life. Freud writes: "The processes [of the unconscious] are atemporal, that is to say that they are not ordered temporally, are not modified by the passing of time, have absolutely no relation to time."[170] It is for this reason that the infantile desires continue to disturb the life of the adult.

Freud explained the psychological origin of faith, this kind of oceanic feeling of a communion with the whole, resulting in an impression of eternity. This feeling comes from the condition of the infant, in whose mind the self is not distinguished from the id nor from the external reality. The self includes all. Later, the very young child manages to distinguish his self from reality and to recognize its limits, as well spatial as temporal[171]. This feeling of eternity or immortality, exceptionally developed at Jesus, resulted from a vast megaprojection of the id. In full

---

170. FREUD (Sigmund), *Metapsychology. The unconscious*, part V, "The particular properties of the ICS system", in *Œuvres complètes. Psychoanalysis*, Paris, PUF, 1988, volume XIII, p. 226.
171. See FREUD (Sigmund), "Le malaise dans la culture", in *Œuvres complètes. Psychoanalysis*, Paris, PUF, 1994, volume XVIII, pp. 249-253.

phase with his id, through the absence of opposition from his superego, Jesus let himself be carried on the wave of his atemporal impulses. He continually took a bath in the collective unconscious. He lost himself entirely in it, and transposed the structures of the unconscious onto reality. He hallucinated an atemporal supra-reality, with which he identified himself.

His messianic delusion, based on megaprojections, is also explained. Jesus had unrestricted access to his collective unconscious, in particular to the archetype of the father. On the other hand, not knowing the internal opposition between ego and superego, he could present himself as speaking in the name of God. His overinflated ego made him a real walking superego. Jesus took on the role of a father who gives advice to all. He spoke as a collective superego. Instead of simply submitting to the social rules integrated in his superego, he invented them himself from his collective unconscious. He imposed them on others, with aggressiveness and tenacity.

The delusion of plagiarism derives from the preceding process. We have seen that Jesus feared that others would seduce the crowds by projecting his own case onto others. With his megalomaniacal conviction of being a prophet, he feared that others might produce megaprojections, and take themselves for him.

After the delusions of persecution and grandeur, here is the last of the three most important delusions of Jesus: his delusion of filiation.

The first aspect of this delusion lies in his claim to be "son of God":

"[...] my Father who is in heaven [...]"[172]

To understand this first delusion, which will then become interwoven in a systematized development, it is enough to refer

---

172. *Matthew* (7:21), (16:17).

to the notion of "father" in psychoanalysis. The father represents authority, the "superior", the laws. But Jesus felt that his father was different, he was not a simple father, not this humble carpenter. His megalomania would not have been satisfied with that. He felt in him a greater being, a universal father. As a good mega-paranoid, Jesus felt the archetypal, the collective unconscious, in himself. He believed he had laws for all. By attributing this interiority to the heavens, he made a megaprojection. A mistake, certainly, but a great one.

Many of Jesus' statements implicitly confirm this interpretation of the father in terms of archetypal laws:

"When you have lifted up the Son of Man, then you will know what I am, and that I do nothing of myself, but speak as the Father has taught me. He who sent me is with me; he has not left me alone, because I always do what is pleasing to him."[173]

The last aspect, "doing what is pleasing to him", is funda-mental. Jesus not only felt the archetype of the universal father within him, with its collective laws. Moreover, and this is a deci-sive characteristic, he was in communion with these laws. Unlike normally constituted people, he did not feel the universal laws as a constraint. He got along with his father, one might say. This is again the motif of the permuted superego, stemming from the reversed Oedipus complex. Instead of entering into conflict with the father, he nourished a loving relationship with him. He loved him, and felt loved in return. This is the secret of Jesus' happiness, his true paradise: the absence of ego-on-ego tension.

"It is my Father who glorifies me [...]"[174]

A final step remains to be taken in order to unravel part of the mystery of Jesus, namely what he brought to the crowd that was

---

173. *John* (8:28-29).
174. *John* (8:54).

original. By megaprojection, he proposed to transpose his own positive relationship to the father to the one the crowd was to have with him. Happy to be in tune with his unconscious father, he proposed to the crowd to establish the same relationship with him, his earthly representative:

"As the Father has loved me, so I have loved you. Remain in my love. If you keep my commandments, you will abide in my love, just as I have kept my Father's commandments, and abide in his love."[175]

Jesus proposed at the same time the end of bad conscience and obedience. He proposed the love of laws, which hardly weighed on him, since he gave them to himself. He presented himself as a model. He brought to light the loving aspect of the father to the son, which was a novelty compared to the repressive side of the Jewish tradition (such as the restrictive injunctions of Moses).

"You are my friends if you do what I command you. [...] What I command you is to love one another."[176]

From then on, love itself became the content of his order. By megaprojection, the supreme law of Jesus required to be like him, in love with the father. He was moving towards his delusional system, which is a transposition of himself: within himself, love of self. On the level of his community, the same dichotomy appeared, by megaprojection: inside the community, love of self, that is, love of one another (but correlatively, hatred of people outside the community). Jesus proposed to the community what he felt in himself: unity through love, love of the common law, of the father shared by all, that is, of himself, Jesus. He wanted everyone to love him, as he loved himself, and as he felt his father loved him. It is incredible: he ordered the crowd, in a barely

---

175. *John* (15:9-10).
176. *John* (15:14, 17).

disguised way, "love me"... And some of the crowd loved him. We will have to try to understand why they fell in love with such a tyrannical being and why they wanted to obey his laws...

The peace announced by Jesus contains the same ambiguity as for love. This peace, between man and God, is the megaprojection of the psychotic fusion between the ego and the superego of Jesus. On the other hand, Jesus announced the war. From the point of view of consciousness, this is contradictory. But in the unconscious, aggressive (death) and love (life) impulses are inextricably linked. Jesus loved and attacked his listeners at the same time, assuming the ambivalent role of the father. Moreover, as a good psychotic, he never turned his aggression on himself, reserving it for others, for the outside world. Two possibilities were open to him. Either his listeners obeyed him. They would then enter the Christian community, and become illusorily unified thanks to his identical love for all. Or his listeners disobeyed him, in which case they attracted his hatred, his threats, his vindictiveness, etc. They then found themselves at the mercy of the Church. They would then find themselves outside the Christian community and exposed to many inconveniences. This pathological mechanism, which originated with Jesus, was perpetuated in later Christian history, with the inquisition or the excommunications, not forgetting the crusades.

When Jesus gave the first commandment to love God, and incidentally not to blaspheme against him, he was the first beneficiary, he who identified himself with God, in the schizophrenic Trinity. This order denoted an immense vanity, although insidiously veiled.

From this curious father-son relationship, this inverted relationship that is love and internalization of laws, flowed this astonishing advice that Jesus kept repeating about childhood:

"I tell you the truth, whoever does not receive the kingdom of God as a little child will not enter it."[177]

What does this image mean? To know happiness, in other words to receive the love of the father and no longer be in conflict with the laws, one would have to become a child, as Jesus himself was. This implies that one should no longer feel a bad conscience, a conflict between the laws of the superego and the self. One would have to have a superego that functions in reverse, without hateful reproaches towards oneself. It would be necessary to be Jesus, "innocent". In other words: psychotic.

This love for one another, as a transposition of his attachment to himself, followed a natural inclination, which is that of love in general: the fusion between two beings. This is the second aspect of Jesus' delusion of filiation.

Love fused the two beings, which literally interpenetrated:

"The Father is in me and I am in the Father."[178]

In his sick mind, only one being resulted:

"I and the Father are one."[179]

Here is a megaparanoid delusion, in all its purity, which requires an explanation, like a serious pathology. Now that the psychological mechanisms have come to light, clarification seems more accessible. This is the "psychotic fusion". Jesus merged his ego with his super-ego. And his delusions of grandeur only aggravated this unnatural union, to become a megalomaniacal fusion between his small self and the great archetypal superego of his collective unconscious, which contains universal laws.

This internal fusion of Jesus was in turn transposed to his relationship with the crowd:

---

177. *Luke* (18:17), see also *Matthew* (18:3), (19:14), *Mark* (10:13-16).
178. *John* (10:38).
179. *John* (10:30).

"I have made your name known to them, and I will make it known to them, that the love with which you loved me may be in them, and I in them."[180]

Jesus had become one with himself, through psychotic fusion. All internal tension had disappeared in him. By transposition, the same process was to be applied to the multitude, which was supposed to become one in its turn. This was another mega-projection on the part of Jesus, who expanded the dreamlike delusion of the Trinity to include the crowd:

"I have given them the glory that you have given me, so that they may be one as we are one - I in them, and you in me - so that they may be perfectly one, and the world may know that you have sent me and loved them as you have loved me."[181]

The third aspect of the delusion of filiation, so prominent in Jesus, was the curious appellation "Son of Man". This was supposed to emphasize the human character of Jesus, which contradicted his divine aspect. To be human is to be here on earth; to be divine is to be up there in heaven. Some might possibly reply that he was temporarily human, for the time of his incarnation. However, these after-the-fact arrangements are nothing more than tinkering on a building without foundations, that is to say, on a series of myths.

On the other hand, if "divine" means "in psychotic fusion with the collective superego", then human and divine are no longer contradictory. Jesus was indeed a man, with a very particular mental configuration. His superego and his ego were one. He had access to the collective unconscious. He felt in him the universal, the human in general. He believed to incarnate humanity, the "phylogenetic" (what belongs to the species in general). To call

180. *John* (17:26).
181. *John* (17:22-23).

himself "Son of Man", as a human being in general, means that he understood in himself the general structures of humanity. His ego was inflated, to reach the status of collective ego, by fusion with the collective father, which lies in the unconscious. This megaparanoid configuration remaining extremely rare, Jesus could pass for supernatural or divine in the eyes of ordinary men.

The difficulty now consists in explaining these mythical projections, by bringing to light their unconscious keys.

Most of Jesus' declamations were full of words that do not refer to anything real. Expressions such as "God," "eternal life," "sanctification," "heavenly food," did not refer to anything in reality. In fact, they were unintentional allusions to unconscious facts or factors. When a Christian believes in the reality of these entities, he is simply fooling a myth. And he who invents a myth is a megaparanoid. He makes them up by producing mythical projections. Such was Jesus.

A systematic translation becomes necessary to understand what each of his parables really means, from the point of view of the unconscious. The keys to these translations, from delirious language to psychological reality, are these words. Here are some illustrations of how to decipher these keys.

First of all, a few words used by Jesus, which he only took from the Jewish tradition:

The word "God" is attached to all its derivatives, albeit in a psychological sense. The "kingdom of God" would designate a place, a paradise, where reconciliation with the father would be complete, a space without tension between self and superego. This utopia, of unconscious origin, is also at the source of the myth of the golden age, where any desire is immediately realized, without prohibition, without physical impossibility. On the real level, such a psychological configuration can be realized in two ways. Firstly, happiness exists in a way at the time when ego and superego are not yet formed. Freud calls this the "primary narcissism". This corresponds to the age of the fetus or the young infant, without internal psychological tension between two instances that do not yet exist, the ego and the superego. As soon as these two authorities are formed, by identification with the parents, the tension of the parental injunctions against the desires of the self becomes permanent. Except in the case of the psychotic, whose self and superego function in opposite mode. Instead of being opposed, his superego expresses love for his self, from where results their fusion. It is the second way to realize psychologically the myth of the golden age. It is a special case, very minority in the population, that Freud calls "secondary narcissism", another name of the psychosis. In general, the meeting between these psychotics and healthy men is stormy, as these patients ignore the external constraints, coming from society. In short, paradise is the mythical projection of primary narcissism, made by a psychotic.

We can apply this conclusion, to discover what the "eternal punishment" symbolizes (the eternal punishments, the divine punishment), by mirror effect. This one simply represents the opposite of the psychotic fusion: the megaprojection of the never resolved, inevitable tension between the poor self and the tyrannical superego. As soon as an impulse acts, that is to say almost always, anguish and bad conscience appear.

The "law of God", the "divine justice", etc., designate the conformity to the socioreligious orders integrated in the superego. The problem lies in the fact that the ego-self mold can integrate any kind of laws. To change these always remains possible. The ego-self mold is an empty structure, a shell, which can be filled with any contents. It can be the laws of a State, integrated by the citizen, the religious dogmas, assimilated by the believer and invented by a megaparanoid, or even the rules of a group of thugs, that each of its representatives respects.

The illusion of divine law occurs when a subject attributes these laws to a Being who would exist in the sky. Good and evil, illusions par excellence, are added to it. The good is supposed to designate the adequacy with the divine verb. In other words, it derives from a megaprojection of conformity with the inner voice of the collective superego. And evil, as Freud indicates about the devil, represents the impulses of the id[182]. If you believe in the actual existence of good and evil, you are making a megaprojection by attributing to reality simple unconscious mechanisms. You wrongly objectify a simple relation between unconscious operators. If you make a character of it, it will be an anthropomorphism. You attribute an almost human form to what is devoid of it, a place of the unconscious.

If you obey the laws of your superego, in other words if it manages to contain the desires coming from your id, you are acting "well". If not, you are committing a "sin". It is a simple illusion, resulting from the fact that certain unconscious desires overflow the superego, whether you want it or not. Sin could only exist if man were free to choose his actions. But as Freud says, "the ego is not master in its own house"[183]. The unconscious determines our acts without our knowledge. "Instrument of your body, such is also your little reason that you call 'mind', my brother, a little instrument and plaything of

---

182. See FREUD (Sigmund), " Caractère et érotisme anal ", in *Névrose, psychose et perversion*, Paris, PUF, 1992.
183. FREUD (Sigmund), "Une difficulté de la psychanalyse", in *Œuvres complètes. Psychoanalysis*, Paris, PUF, 1996, volume XV, p. 50.

your great reason."[184] This real absence of free will is moreover itself projected, in a mythical way, by religion, in the notions of "God's grace", "election", "predestination", etc. Obviously, religious people contradict themselves on this point, since on the one hand they claim to be free, and on the other hand that everything is already written.

There is a metaphor that illustrates these matters of good and evil, like an unconscious motif that runs underground throughout the mythical imagery of Jesus. It is "purity". To be "pure" is to be washed of one's faults, which is represented by this curious notion of "atonement". Jesus projects his anal character, which separates the pure from the impure, onto moral questions, onto the relationship between the self and the superego. Purity becomes the projection of the particular case where self and superego are not in opposition.

Jesus did not invent this myth, but developed it further, especially with "sanctification", making the "saint" someone "pure and separate". The saint, on the model of Jesus, would be an untainted and unmixed person, which represents a reaction of opposition to the strong infantile penchant for excrement. The saint is a simple religious symbolization of this, by projection onto the moral plane of the inverted superego of Jesus, who judged himself as good.

The belief in spirits is a very basic mythical projection. It consists in attributing thoughts to objects or even to reality in general. The kind of thoughts attributed to these objects determines the kind of spirits to which the believers give credit. If these thoughts are "evil" (from the id), then demons appear, and if these thoughts are validated by the superego, angels appear.

184. NIETZSCHE (Friedrich), *Thus Spoke Zarathustra*, part I, "Of the Contemptors of the Body", Paris, Gallimard, 1947, p. 44.

The artificial distinction between "soul" and "body" is itself the result of a mythical projection. Freud explains that this separation comes from the projection of the distinction between consciousness and unconscious[185].

Blasphemy" is a funny kind of sin. Blasphemy is no longer just contradicting God's laws, but directly attacking his source, God himself. It is the direct manifestation of the Oedipus complex, which symbolically realizes the desire to kill the father. The blasphemy refers to this prohibition internalized in the superego, with its counterpart, the incestuous desire.

The "truth of God" and the "mystery of God", or the "divine omniscience" which remains inaccessible to the consciousness of the common man, refer to the fact that the unconscious contains all the knowledge of the subject.

The famous "inspiration", or "enthusiasm" (etymologically "God in us"), metaphorically represents the ascent of the structures of the collective unconscious to consciousness.

Jesus also took up the notion of "messiah", which designates an envoy of God whose mission is to free the world from evil. His very special personality had everything to meet the popular expectation: a sense of superiority, purity and greatness, and an obsession with saving the world. He took on this messiah archetype, as if it had been tailor-made for him. This mega-projection, inherited from tradition, crystallized what he felt confusedly about himself.

Most of these mythical notions were taken up by Jesus. Here are a few more of his own.

---

185. FREUD (Sigmund), *Totem and Taboo*, chapter III, "Animism, magic and omnipotence of ideas", part IV, in *Œuvres complètes. Psychoanalysis*, Paris, PUF, 1998, volume XI, pp. 303-304.

CHAPTER IV: THE MEGAPARANOIA OF JESUS

One of the most important is "forgiveness", as opposed to the capital "law of retaliation". Instead of returning an eye for an eye, a tooth for a tooth, we should now turn the other cheek. Jesus reversed the punitive relationship of God to man, of the collective superego to the self. He created a myth from the projection of his own unconscious structure.

That it was Jesus who projected the parental function of forgiveness, this archetype of the collective unconscious, is understandable. His superego and his ego were not in conflict. He megaprojected, in an illusory supra-reality, a simple dysfunction of his pathological unconscious. He developed a hypersensitivity to the particular moment of the reconciliation of the father with the child, the forgiveness. Indeed, he himself was unaware of the torturous tension of the bad conscience, that permanent confrontation between a normally repressive superego and the ego. Instead of punishing him, his superego encouraged him; rather than preventing him from performing acts prohibited by society, it "forgave" him. The unconscious of Jesus functioned as a machine for erasing faults, for "purifying".

Jesus claimed to "save from sin". The name Jesus means "Yahweh saves". This important parental function had remained in the background until Jesus. The Jewish God was mostly feared for his laws and his wrath. Jesus, who was unconsciously loved by his superego, dwelt on this other paternal aspect. The father, at the same time as he scolds and represses, loves and protects. Jesus emphasized this second, more sympathetic side, by mythical projection of his own inverted relationship between ego and superego. Part of his success is explained by the fact that he focuses on the positive side of the father.

The social reversal promoted by Jesus, which is also a mythical projection, is equally interesting.

"Thus the last shall be first, and the first shall be last."[186]

Jesus kept a dog of his bitch to the rich. This hatred referred to the Oedipus complex. Jesus promised a bad fate to those who dominate. The rich symbolize a constraining father in opposition to the self. This paradise promised by Jesus is in this sense a place where the self ceases to have a superior, a repressive superego. It is still the myth of the golden age. That the poor come first, by reversing the social order, amounts to overthrowing the father, and to realizing the Oedipal desire to kill the rulers. What harm can the rich do? In Jesus' unconscious, it is quite simple: they are impure, they are tainted by the excremental symbol of money. Jesus dedicated all the hatred of his aggressive impulses to those who had not sublimated their attraction to money, itself derived from the interest in excrement. In other words, it was necessary, like him, to have sublimated twice. It was again a transposition of his own internal relationships onto social relationships in general. His psychotic structure made him a megalomaniac rebel who could not stand any superior.

The notion of "resurrection" is a mythical projection of the id as a whole. We have said that the unconscious ignores time. In the id, we are eternal, which is what Jesus projected into reality. Even if he himself did not invent this bedtime story, his spirit was no less respected. In the myth of the resurrection we find a certain taste for the negation of the passage of time, which characterizes the functioning of the unconscious, and even more so of the collective unconscious.

Jesus had made another megaprojection, which was very important to him. This is his famous "good news", the happiness he announced to the "blessed". In reality, this well-being comes from the unconscious, as attested by the fact that it is promised to

---

186. *Matthew* (20:1-16).

heaven. According to the results of the analysis of the Jesus case, this happiness was his own, internal happiness. It represents the absence of tension between ego and superego, the fact of merging with the archetype of the father, and of being one's own master. This is the good news that Jesus announced: there is a universe where men live happily, without fault or bad conscience... it is that of one's own unconscious - a psychotic universe.

The above psychological mechanisms should make it possible to examine some of the strange parables of Jesus, which are in fact allegorical allusions to certain structures and other archetypes of the collective unconscious. In particular, they propose symbolic satisfactions to all the sources of infantile pleasure, unconscious in the adult, according to their three stages.

For the oral stage, let's start with this strange delusion of Jesus:
"I am the bread of life. Your fathers ate the manna in the desert and died. This is the bread that comes down from heaven, so that whoever eats it will not die. I am the living bread that came down from heaven. If anyone eats of this bread, he will live forever; and the bread that I will give is my flesh, which I will give for the life of the world. The Jews were discussing this among themselves, saying: How can he give us his flesh to eat? Jesus said unto them, Verily, verily, I say unto you, Except ye eat the flesh of the Son of man, and drink his blood, ye have no life in yourselves. He who eats my flesh and drinks my blood has eternal life, and I will raise him up at the last day. For my flesh is food indeed, and my blood is drink indeed. He who eats my flesh and drinks my blood abides in me, and I in him. As the living Father sent me, and I live because of the Father, so he who eats me will live because of me. This is the bread that came down from heaven. It is not like your fathers who ate the manna and died: he who eats this bread will live forever."[187]

---

187. *John* (6:48-58), see also *Matthew* (26:26-28).

Freud explains these paradoxical statements:

"In the Christian myth, man's hereditary sin is undoubtedly a sin committed against God the Father. If, therefore, Christ acquits mankind of the burden of hereditary sin by sacrificing his own life, then he forces us to the conclusion that this sin was a murderous act. According to the law of retaliation, deeply rooted in human sensibility, a murder can only be atoned for by sacrificing another life; self-sacrifice refers to a bloodshed. And if the sacrifice one makes of one's own life leads to reconciliation with God the Father, the crime to be expiated could not be other than the murder perpetrated on the father."[188]

Freud's explanation is clear. It allows to open the following developments. Jesus was in internal reconciliation, his superego and his ego were not in opposition. But he proposed the same "contract", which he signed with his father, to his disciples. He wanted to insinuate himself into them as his father had entered into him, that is, positively. He proposed his own inverted Oedipal relationship to his disciples, by making himself their "integrated" father.

This symbolic oddity, which constitutes a delusion derived from the collective structures of the unconscious, enabled Jesus to gain credibility with his listeners on several levels. By giving his life as a son, he immediately fascinated men with a reprobate superego. He relieved their dark conscience, erasing their unconscious fault, namely the desire to kill the father. By doing so, he intruded into their unconscious: he proposed to feed them and to die for them. It is the oral stage. Not content with having erased the oedipal fault, he allowed it to be satisfied with impunity. To eat a Jesus who

188. FREUD (Sigmund), *Totem and Taboo*, chapter III, "Animism, magic and the omnipotence of ideas", part IV, in *Complete Works. Psychoanalysis, op. cit.* Volume XI, p. 374.

gives his life and assumes the role of master, was for the disciple to kill another father - Jesus himself - who pretended to abandon any negatively superior and constraining aspect, an absolutely sympathetic father, ideal for the unconscious, a father already killed. He kept only the pleasant aspect of the father, the love. He was a father "ready to love", perfect for a fusion between the ego and the superego. It was good news, a prospect of timeless happiness.

Jesus was doing double duty. He was giving his son's life to relieve the father's unconscious desire to kill. And he was proposing to the disciple, by being eaten, to integrate in himself his own positive relationship with the father. This mechanism makes it possible to clarify the meaning of sentences of this kind:

"This is how the Son of Man came [...] to [...] give his life as a ransom for many."[189]

A third unconscious register was added: Jesus also made himself a mother, with the myth of eternal food, as a repressed memory of the abundant breast. He thus played on all the unconscious levels.

Jesus symbolically satisfied the first stage of man, the oral stage, which he enhanced with an Oedipal satisfaction, both on the father's and the mother's side. It promised food for ever. But after having eaten well, the moment of the dejection comes. Just as after the oral stage comes the sadistic-anal stage, a stage where the very young child takes pleasure in defiling the objects of his entourage, and himself.

"Look at the birds of the air; they neither sow nor reap, nor do they gather into barns; and your heavenly Father feeds them. Are you not worth much more than they?"[190]

Jesus forbade the accumulation of money. This was violently at odds with a social context that highly valued money and

---

189. *Matthew* (20:28).
190. *Matthew* (6:26).

commerce. Jesus had to offer some kind of compensation to satisfy his audience. The solution was simple, he had to propose an eternal satisfaction of economic needs, at their root, in the unconscious. The detour of sublimation, "in heaven", allows to satisfy this fascination for wealth, which in the unconscious corresponds to the infantile pleasure of the retention of stools. Jesus proposed an eternal satisfaction of the need for moral righteousness and desires of a sadistic-anal order, by means of a double sublimation, from excrement to money, and then from money to heaven.

He who accepts the teaching of Jesus is always full. He rises with Jesus in the double sublimation of the anal stage: Jesus hated real impurity as much as symbolic impurity, money. He demanded the same of his disciples, transforming once again into a universal order what was only valid for his unconscious functioning. He always attached the fault, the defilement, to anal productions. Having doubly sublimated this stage, he proposed in exchange an immaterial good: his happy unconscious, his positive superego. But how to proceed ?

The answer is in the parable, implicitly. The fact that Jesus speaks of a heavenly Father who "feeds" the birds, represents a path to follow. Here we find the motif of heavenly, and therefore eternal, food. Jesus had given himself as food. He wanted to be assimilated instead of earthly food, as a source of superior and infinite happiness. The accumulation of money became useless; instead, it was his teaching that had to be accumulated. Once this enrichment was digested, it was not to be rejected, as another parable shows:

"It is not what goes into the mouth that defiles the man; but what comes out of the mouth, that defiles the man."[191]

---

191. *Matthew* (15:11).

The body separated from the soul designates the id distinct from the ego, the unconscious from the consciousness. The body as a whole produces excrement (or vomit). In other words, the devalued body referred to the id judged as dirty. It had to undergo the purification of Jesus. How could he curb the desires of the id, especially those stemming from the anal character, desires of impurity and destruction?

In the unconscious, eating and killing come back to the same thing. The infant, who devours on the phantasmatic mode the mother's breast, eats her. The myth of the cannibalism comes from it, the supreme fault consisting in killing the father, by eating him. To eat the father to destroy him, it is to acquire his power. Once digested, excrements come out, symbolized by money - this one being dirty, and therefore at fault according to Jesus. The latter forbade letting out what had entered the mouth. What entered the mouths of his disciples?

It was himself, again, that is, his teachings, especially his positive internal relationship between his superego and his self. What entered the disciple's mouth was Jesus as a walking superego.

He entered the bodies of his followers to purify them, that is, to cleanse their faults, and never to come out as excrement, or money, or power. He entered their superego to control them from within and force them to remain small. His listeners had to obey him because they had incorporated him into their superego, just as Jesus' ego was located in his own superego, identified with God.

By eating Jesus, as a father figure, the disciple was supposed to be able to become his own father, like Jesus. Thus, it was necessary to eat the spiritual teaching of Jesus, to preserve it, and to spit out the earthly, impure foods.

After having satisfied, unconsciously and in a symbolic way, the oral stage and then the sadistic-anal stage of the listener,

Jesus proposed to replace the satisfactions of the third, phallic stage as well.

"If your hand or your foot is a stumbling block to you, cut it off and throw it away; it is better for you to enter life lame or one-handed, than to have two feet or two hands and be thrown into eternal fire. And if your eye is a stumbling block to you, pluck it out and cast it from you; it is better for you to enter life with one eye than to have two eyes and be cast into hellfire.[192]

Nietzsche replies:

"The most famous formula is found in the New Testament, in the "Sermon on the Mount", where, in parentheses, things are not seen *from above*. For example, it says - and this applies to sexuality: "If your eye causes you to sin, pluck it out."[193]

As if to support Nietzsche, Freud affirms that the eye symbolically represents the testicle. To tear out one's eye is to castrate oneself. But here, it is curious to see Jesus proposing to castrate oneself, as a condition for entering paradise rather than hell.

In what way would someone punishing himself access the happiness of internal reconciliation rather than the hell of a bad conscience? In this way, punishing oneself amounts to becoming one's own father, as a castrator, and no longer receiving any external constraint. This act turned over against oneself makes it possible not to feel any more the anguish due to the threat of castration by an external father, symbolic of the punishment of the self by the superego. There again appears the motive of the psychotic fusion of Jesus with himself, which implied not to receive external orders.

---

192. *Matthew* (18:8-9), see also *Mark* (9:42-48).
193. NIETZSCHE (Friedrich), *Crépuscule des Idoles*, "La morale, une anti-nature", § 1, in *Œuvres philosophiques complètes*, Paris, Gallimard-NRF, 1990, tome VIII, p. 82.

There is still a huge difference between Jesus and his disciples that will never be bridged. It lies in the fact that Jesus gave himself his principles, from within, while the others received them from outside, namely from him, Jesus. Castrating oneself was the only way to apply Jesus' advice without being Jesus. It was the only way to keep an illusion of paternal decision, without having given oneself its laws, while no longer fearing punishment, castration. It was a second-hand paradise. An artificial paradise.

Castrating oneself, by integrating Jesus, was tantamount to identifying with an apparently sympathetic father, which allowed one to believe oneself to be a father without having to overthrow another father, without fear of being punished (castrated) by an evil father, since Jesus presented himself as a child. This self-mutilation symbolized the fact that one accepted what Jesus kept asking for: innocence, i.e. an infantile state, where one does not give oneself laws, but without suffering the anguishing weight of laws and punishments.

This mechanism appears clearly in another parable that also uses the eye:

"Why do you see the mote that is in your brother's eye, and do not see the beam that is in your own eye?"[194]

This famous parable was constructed by projection. As a self-respecting paranoid, Jesus was more willing to see the faults of others than his own.

Why did Jesus use these strange symbols, of a straw and a beam, knowing that the eye, as a testicle, represents the claim to be a father?

Straw and beam are phallic symbols, representing the erect penis. The combination of these two symbols denoted the impulses of the id, with the testicle-eye as the source of fatherhood

---

194. *Matthew* (7:3).

and the beam-phallus as the means of the sexual act. Knowing that Jesus advised to castrate oneself rather than to commit a fault, he seemed to order to renounce also the pleasure of coitus.

The phallus, besides being a means of coitus, also represents male pride. This parable evokes the prosaic myth of the biggest phallus as a symbol of increased virility, as domination over other men. To encourage one to look away from the small pride of one's neighbor in order to concentrate on one's own swelling pride, was tantamount to demanding that the most powerful men themselves renounce their superiority in order to become children of Jesus.

"Christianity intends to overcome *wild animals*: its method consists in making them *sick* - weakening is the Christian recipe for *taming*, for "civilization".[195]

Thus Jesus satisfied the oral stage forever by giving himself as eternal food, to compensate for the murder and consumption of the father, while at the same time making himself a foster mother. He satisfied the desires of the sadistic-anal stage by offering to wash away all faults, especially that of killing and defiling. He forbade to accumulate money, ordering to keep it, Jesus, inside oneself (after having eaten it). He forbade the enjoyment of the excrements resulting from the consumption of the killed father. In exchange, he offered a gift (excremental symbol): he offered eternal and pure wealth in exchange for material goods, whose accumulation is always limited. Finally, he satisfied the phallic stage by offering to punish himself, to return to infantile innocence under the guidance of a sympathetic father. In fact, this astonishing action calms the anguish, resulting from the

---

195. Nietzsche (Friedrich), "L'Antéchrist", in *Œuvres philosophiques complètes, op. cit.* Volume VIII, § 22, p. 179.

CHAPTER IV: THE MEGAPARANOIA OF JESUS

unconscious fear of a paternal reprimand, namely the fear to be castrated by the father, for having desired the mother.

To put it even more succinctly, Jesus proposed to give oneself food in order to obtain a positive relationship with the father, to keep only oneself as a positive internal relationship, rejecting material goods, and finally to castrate any desire to make oneself a father or a powerful person in turn. The admirable unity of these three levels of satisfaction is obvious. In each case, Jesus symbolically proposed reconciliation with the father. He was removing the guilty conscience associated with each of these repressed desires. By taking on the role of a mother, he solved the triangular problem of the Oedipus complex: a father killed with impunity, an infinitely generous mother, an innocent child. Better than the Holy Trinity, Jesus alone constituted an Oedipal trilogy.

One argument, which may cool down the zealots of the Immaculate Conception somewhat, is to note that another realization of the Oedipus complex appears in the Gospels, for a reader who would strategically connect some of Jesus' delusional convictions. If he existed before his birth[196], if he and the father were one[197], and if his mother Mary was born by the Holy Spirit... Fortunately for Jesus, this invention of maternal virginity is probably not to be put on his account, which is otherwise sufficiently charged.

Another series of parables is more abstract, more sublime. These parables are based on the metaphor of light. The light represents "conscience", in the two senses of "moral conscience" and "way of seeing the world". Jesus was indeed changing reality, offering a different way of looking at things and a different light. He claimed to be the light of the world, and claimed to avoid

---

196. *John* (8:58), see also *Matthew* (19:29), (26:32).
197. *John* (14:9-11), see also *John* (16:15).

darkness for those who followed him[198]. He considered the universe from his own unconscious structures. He looked at it by hallucinating it. He transformed the world into a waking dream.

The light designated the conscience, the spirit, the reason, the good, etc. In contrast, darkness represented evil, the id (during sleep, in the dark, the impulses come up, the ego fades away). What was the light that he claimed to bring? Of which good did he speak? A relaxation due to an absence of guilt. In addition to this inner peace, Jesus brought new religious rules, the "good ones", making himself a higher consciousness. The light also referred to the truth allegedly produced by his conscience.

"If you abide in my word, you are truly my disciples; you will know the truth, and the truth will set you free."[199]

What truth did he bring? That of his positive oedipal relationship. In fact, Jesus gave access to the unconscious by the detour of the symbol. His "truth" designated the inverted superego of his unconscious, which liberated... from bad conscience. "I am the light of the world" was the symbolic way Jesus used to say that he was the moral conscience for all. We have already mentioned another parable, which used the motif of the light in a curious way[200]. In it Jesus said that the one who lights the lamp does not hide it. In so doing, he was pointing to himself, who was supposed to see and know better than anyone else. He thought he saw the kingdom of God and its laws. He showed this light to others, allowing them to "see" in turn. He presented his truths, which came from his collective unconscious, and then applied them to reality, to transfigure it in a delirious way.

---

198. *John* (8:12).
199. *John* (8:31-32).
200. *Luke* (8:16-18).

In the same parable, Jesus went on to suggest that nothing hidden would remain hidden. He thought he was evoking God's gaze, but it was his superego he was acting out.

This was followed by the mysterious phrase that one gives to the one who has, and takes away from the one who thinks he has. The one who has the light of Jesus, his piercing conscience in a way, will have the paradise. This kingdom of heaven refers to the happiness of the positive fusion ego-on-ego and to the eternity of the unconscious, finally accessible by megaprojection. The one who does not have consciousness will not have paradise, he will have nothing at all, especially not his wealth. He will only have the bad conscience of a superego opposed to the id, with the painful consequences of repression.

Finally, Jesus claimed that it was possible to move or remove a mountain by the sheer force of faith[201]. Galvanized Christians of ancient times may have tried this, but today they would probably agree that it is only an image.

Metaphorically, this upheaval of reality through faith has a real unconscious meaning. With faith, the universe seemed different. It added a being behind the world: God. It was a radical change. In particular, at the cost of this mythical projection, life acquired a meaning. Faith really changed the believer's outlook. To see as Jesus would be to accept his good news, the end of faults. For men tortured by their bad conscience, the universe would really change.

This phenomenon is only due to an unconscious mechanism, alas!

If the understanding of the case of Jesus has progressed, the mystery of his success with the crowds has thickened. At the confluence of schizophrenia and anal retentivity, Jesus proved to

---

201. *Matthew* (21:21-22), *Mark* (11:22-24).

be profoundly paranoid - even mega-paranoid, since his megalo-mania generated mythical projections.

But then, how could such a great delusional person have any impact on the crowd? He communicated in an obscure mode, he was aggressive and delusional on a grand scale... Moreover, how did the crowd picture Jesus as he was not, i.e., conforming to the values he defended without practicing them?

Chapter V:
Cured Hysterics

An atheist could easily reject the veracity of Jesus' healings on the grounds that they seem inexplicable. He would save himself a reflection on a serious problem: how could Jesus have healed so many sick people by simply talking to them?

By such an attitude, this atheist would also show bad faith. There are many testimonies, from different sources, about many similar facts. Just as the historical existence of Jesus cannot be denied, his healings did exist, at least in part. Here is a mystery that an atheist has to explain concretely, if he wants to deny that Jesus is the son of God.

According to the Gospels, Jesus could heal a "possessed" person:

"There was a man in their synagogue with an unclean spirit, who cried out, 'What have we to do with you, Jesus of Nazareth? You have come to lose us. I know who you are: the Holy One of God. And Jesus rebuked him, saying: Be quiet, and come out of the man. And the unclean spirit came out of the man, shaking him violently and crying out with a loud voice. And all were amazed, so that they asked one another, What is this? A new doctrine! He commands with authority even the unclean spirits, and they obey him! And immediately his fame spread to all the surrounding places of Galilee."[202]

Jesus also seemed to be able to heal an individual's physical ailments:

Jesus answered, "What do you want me to do? Rabouni [Master]," the blind man answered, "that I may receive my sight. And Jesus said to him, "Go, your faith has saved you. Immediately he received his sight and followed Jesus on his way."[203]

And, even better, Jesus seemed to be able to heal ailments on a large scale:

"Wherever he came, in villages, towns or the countryside, they would put the sick in the public squares and ask him to allow them to touch only the edge of his garment. And all who touched him were healed."[204]

Without recourse to God, how can we explain that Jesus was able to heal all those lepers, paralyzed, blind, deaf, demon-possessed, feverish, prostrate, convulsive patients, etc.?

To solve this mystery, Freud's discoveries on hysteria are of precious help. What is hysteria?

Hysteria comprises a pathological tension between superego and ego, like all neuroses. This tension results from the oedipal prohibition concerning the incestuous desires and the asocial desires in general. Once internalized, the ban functions as a permanent pressure on the self. This tension creates on the one hand unconscious conflicts, on the other hand a will to adapt to the social reality. When the neurotic leaves the norm, by his behavior or his words, he feels anguish or bad conscience. He then strives to return to normality.

---

202. *Mark* (1:23-28), see also *Matthew* (17:18), *Luke* (4:33-37), (9:37-43).
203. *Mark* (10:51-53), see also *Matthew* (9:22), *Mark* (5:34), *Luke* (5:18, 20, 24-25).
204. *Mark* (6:56), see also *Matthew* (8:16), (12:15), (19:2), *Mark* (1:33-34), *Luke* (4:40-41).

With hysteria, these unconscious conflicts take a particular way of expression: that of the body. One speaks then about "somatization". The symptoms of hysterics are expressed in a thousand forms, as varied as they are shimmering, but the body is always their means of expression. Hysteria is not a false disease, an imaginary disease. It constitutes a true disease, although of psychological origin.

The fundamental principle is the imitation of a physical illness. At the end of the nineteenth century, hysterics imitated epilepsy on a massive scale. The hysteric of the time would make her big scene of loss of consciousness, epileptic convulsion, with her eyes rolled back and her tongue hanging out, waving her limbs in a disordered way, etc. The hysterics thus imitate a great number of diseases or physical evils. In particular, they develop skin problems, breathing problems, various pains, dysfunction of the limbs, sometimes to the point of paralysis, and deficiency of sensory organs, which can reach blindness or complete deafness, etc.

In all these cases, the imitation is fine enough to deceive neophytes, but not doctors - at least not modern doctors. The latter, thanks to the tests and the superior knowledge of our time, can effectively differentiate a physical disease from a simple hysteria.

This was not the case in Jesus' time.

The personality of the hysteric is marked by this use of the body as a means of pathological expression. In everyday life, theatricality is common. The hysteric puts on a kind of permanent show, dramatizing the most anodyne situations or amplifying the most trivial stories, with forceful gestures and outrageous mimics. He often takes on fairly typical social roles, from animation to theater, through relational jobs, in short everything that implies a physical representation in front of others.

Hysteria is treated well today. Freud found ways to access the unconscious, such as dreams or associations of ideas. These paths allow to reach the psychic causes of physical ailments.

Even before Freud, hypnosis was used. It allowed direct access to the unconscious mind of patients. With a fellow doctor, Breuer, Freud managed to cure the particularly tough symptoms of a patient called Anna O. Hypnosis consisted of putting the subject to sleep, who then dreamed, while fixing his attention on the imperious voice of the hypnotist. The hypnotist literally plays the role of the superego, and suggests false sensations to the patient, as in a dream. In this state, the hypnotized person can access memories that have been repressed from his or her consciousness. He/she remembers the traumatic scenes that caused his/her symptoms. In this case, the hypnotist becomes a real healer, thanks to the psychic ascendancy that the hypnotized person grants him. This particular ascendancy can be compared to that of the superego on the ego. The hypnotist represents the hypnotized person's superego and can act on his unconscious. With this method, Breuer and Freud succeeded in suppressing Anna O.'s pathological symptoms by accessing her traumatic memories. In particular, she developed the curious symptom of a violent disgust for water. They discovered that the origin of this pathological aversion was the fact of having seen a dog drinking from a glass meant for men, a scene she had since forgotten. She had also refused to show her anger and disgust at the time. Under hypnosis, she was able to remember this original trauma, while expressing her previously repressed rage and gagging. From then on, the symptom of disgust for water disappeared forever[205].

---

205. See FREUD (Sigmund) and BREUER (Joseph), *Études sur l'hystérie*, Paris, PUF, coll. "Bibliothèque de psychanalyse", 1992, and for its summary, FREUD (Sigmund), *Cinq leçons sur la psychanalyse*, Paris, Payot, coll. "pbp 84", 1986.

However, hypnosis is very limited. Its effects are only temporary, although spectacular. Other symptoms soon appeared in different forms. For this reason, Freud abandoned hypnosis. He invented a more effective technique in the long term, which goes further back into the unconscious: psychoanalysis...

We can apply the precedents acquired to the supposedly miraculous healings obtained by Jesus. The paralyzed, blind, deaf, demon-possessed, feverish, prostrate, convulsive patients, etc., that he cured were hysterical. Their symptoms were all the result of a somatization of their psychological problems. When the men of that time said "demon-possessed", they were using a metaphor that was not known. It referred to the taking of power by the unconscious over the body, as in sleepwalking. To be "demon-possessed" means that the ego is overwhelmed by the conflicts coming from the id, and cannot control the body anymore...

The case of lepers seems more problematic. Leprosy, being due to a bacillus, is an outright physical disease. There is no chance that Jesus could have really cured such an illness. On the other hand, and this is where the problem lies, it manifests itself as spots on the skin. We can guess that the hysteria of the time must have mimicked leprosy. Today, many skin diseases can have a hysterical origin, like psoriasis, eczema, acne, etc. In other words, Jesus was treating hysterics that mimicked leprosy, not real lepers.

Let us stop for a moment on one of the scenes of supposedly miraculous healing, to better recognize the psychological work of Jesus (our comments are placed in square brackets):

"Master, I have brought to you my son, who is possessed by a mute spirit [translation: an unconscious blockage prevented him from speaking]. Wherever he picks him up, he throws him to the ground; the child foams, grinds his teeth, and becomes all stiff [it was a crisis of hysteria]. [...] And as soon as the child saw Jesus, the spirit agitated him violently [Jesus, with his charisma, impressed the child and his it]; he fell, and rolled on the ground foaming. Jesus asked the father, "How long has this been happening to him? Since he was a child," he answered. And often the spirit has thrown him into the fire and into the water to destroy him. But if you can do anything, come to our rescue, have compassion on us. Jesus said to him, "If you can, all things are possible to him who believes. [The belief in the authority of Jesus was fundamental, it is what allowed hypnosis, not to mention the placebo effect.] Immediately the father of the child cried out: I believe! Come to the rescue of my unbelief! Jesus, seeing the crowd running up, threatened the impure spirit and said to him [the tone was very important, Jesus took a sententious and superior tone, typical of the paranoid, to embody the super-ego of the patient; it was direct hypnosis]: Dumb and deaf spirit, I order you, come out of this child and do not enter it again. And he went out, shouting and shaking him with great violence [this was identical, but with the beliefs of the time, to the work of Breuer and Freud, through hypnosis, on the symptoms of Anna O.]. The child became as if dead, so that many said he was dead [the process being unconscious, the child temporarily lost consciousness]. But Jesus took him by the hand and raised him up. And he stood up."[206]

What the story does not say, of course, is that the effects of hypnosis, as we have noted, are temporary and partial. Freud and Breuer did not give their patient a simple one-time visit.

The mechanism of the miraculous cure was played out by two people. On the one hand, a hysterical victim of unconscious conflicts, on the other hand, a natural hypnotist, who used his charisma to enter into direct communication with the patient's id, like a walking superego. It was a kind of minute psychotherapy.

---

206. *Mark* (9:17-29).

Today, such "healers" are still at work, especially in Black Africa. They are the equivalent of medieval exorcists. But if a Westerner, rational as well as atheistic, goes to see them, there is little hope for his cholesterol level or his diabetes. These healers, like Jesus, can only treat, and rarely cure, psychosomatic diseases that are sensitive to hypnotic suggestion. To obtain a result with a hysteric, two conditions must be met: to have a charismatic healer, and to believe *a priori* in his myths. A megaparanoid is ideal.

At that time, some gullible people could believe very deeply in the myths invented by Jesus. In the West, this is no longer the case. Nowadays, the origin of psychosomatic illnesses is all too well known. Doctors look for the cause where it lies: in the unconscious, not in the sky. It is not surprising that the West no longer heals like Jesus. In spite of all her good will and charisma, Mother Teresa could never be satisfied with saying to genuine lepers "get up, you are cured".

But the adventure of the cure did not stop there. Because of their very demonstrative personalities, the cured hysterics would go everywhere to proclaim what had happened to them. The healer benefited from a kind of natural publicity:

"His fame spread more and more, and people came in droves to hear him and to be cured of their diseases."[207]

These mechanisms constitute a first element to explain Jesus' success. In his time, these healings seemed miraculous. The natural causes, which are the mechanisms of the unconscious, were not known.

In short, a megaparanoid on the one hand, and hysterics on the other, generate apparently miraculous healings and publicity to boot. But it is a long way from crowds believing in the megalomaniacal delusions of Jesus, expressed in demanding and

---

207. *Luke* (5:15), see also *Luke* (4:36-37).

aggressive esoteric language. And how could the crowds see in
Jesus the incarnation of the qualities he advocated, when he was
significantly lacking in them?

Chapter VI: Obsessive Neurotic Sheep

As the Gospels testify, Jesus seemed to have a special charisma. His words literally bewitched the gullible listener. His power of conviction could win over a man, or a few men, face to face:

Then Jesus said to Simon, "Do not be afraid; from now on you will be a fisher of men. And when they had brought the boats to land, they left everything and followed him."[208]

When it is written that they followed him, it was no small commitment:

"Peter [said to Jesus], 'Even if I should die with you, I will not deny you. And all the disciples said the same thing."[209]

Even the people who were *supposedly* hostile and in charge of arresting him fell under his deleterious spell:

"So the officers returned to the chief priests and the Pharisees. And they said to them: Why didn't you bring him? The officers

---

208. *Luke* (5:10-11), see also *Matthew* (4:20), (4:22), (9:9), *Mark* (1:16-20), (2:14), *Luke* (18:28).
209. *Matthew* (26:35).

answered, "Never has a man spoken like this man: No man ever spoke like this man."[210]

Jesus seemed to be able to convey his greatest delusions:

He said to them, "And you, who do you say that I am? Simon Peter answered, "You are the Christ, the Son of the living God."[211]

From then on, the prospect of seducing entire crowds was open to him. The prior arrival of his disciples was like the preparation of a star's tour. Indeed, Jesus did not disdain, on occasion, some spectacular effects:

"A large crowd gathered around him, so he got into a boat and sat down. The whole crowd was standing on the shore."[212]

From then on, he did with the crowd what he did with a few:

"After Jesus had finished these discourses, the crowd was amazed at his doctrine; for he taught as one having authority, and not as their scribes."[213]

"[...] all the people listened to him with admiration."[214]

Once the "snowball effect" started, his reputation preceded him:

"When he entered Jerusalem, the whole city was moved, and they said, 'Who is this? And the people said, 'This is Jesus the prophet, from Nazareth of Galilee."[215]

So much so that Jesus no longer needed to go to the crowds:

"Jesus withdrew to the sea with his disciples. A great multitude followed him from Galilee; and from Judea, and from Jerusalem, and from Idumaea, and from beyond the Jordan, and from

---

210. *John* (7: 45-46).
211. *Matthew* (16:15-16), see also *John* (8:30).
212. *Matthew* (13:2-3).
213. *Matthew* (7:28-29), see also *Luke* (4:31-32).
214. *Luke* (19:48), see also *Mark* (12:37).
215. *Matthew* (21:10-11).

around Tyre and Sidon, a great multitude, hearing all that he did, came to him."[216]

And finally, the glory:

"Jesus, clothed with the power of the Spirit, returned to Galilee, and his fame spread throughout the surrounding country. He taught in the synagogues and was praised by all."[217]

Under these conditions, our question comes back with insistence: how could Jesus have seduced first a few individuals, then crowds, and finally generations and generations of men, who knew him only through his reported words?

To make progress in the investigation of the success of Jesus, Freud left us an extremely valuable key. He declared: "Religion would be the universal constraint neurosis of humanity; like that of the child, it would be the result of the Oedipus complex, of the relationship to the father."[218] We must then direct our research by asking ourselves in what this "neurosis of constraint", also called "obsessional neurosis", consists.

Let's look at its symptoms first[219].

Obsessions are bad thoughts that beset the subject, against his or her will and in an unpleasant way. They can be filthy thoughts, sexual fantasies, murder wishes, etc. The subject implements tactical procedures to ward off these obsessions, procedures that are similar to a magic ritual. The compulsion is an act to which the subject feels compelled although he recognizes it as absurd. He cannot help but perform it repeatedly. The "conjuring" rituals

---

216. *Mark* (3:7-8), see also *Matthew* (13:13), (20:29), *Mark* (2:1-2), (3:20), (8:1), (5:21, 24), *Luke* (4:42), (12:1), (21:38).
217. *Luke* (4:14-15), see also *Matthew* (4:24), *Mark* (11:9-10).
218. FREUD (Sigmund), "The future of an illusion", in *Œuvres complètes. Psychoanalysis*, Paris, PUF, 1994, volume XVIII, p. 184.
219. LEMPERIÈRE (Thérèse) and FÉLINE (André) *et al*, *Adult Psychiatry, op. cit.* chapter IX, "La névrose obsessionnelle".

are based on the impression of the omnipotence of thoughts, as if they could act on the material course of events. This superstition also consists in the belief in invisible entities, usually spirits or powers of action at a distance through thought. They believe in myths with pathological greed.

The objects of these obsessions can be a concrete idea (a word, a thing, a number), or an abstract one (a metaphysical question about life and death, God, etc.), or the subject's behavior (was he right to act that way? did he forget to do something?). These patients have a predilection for undecidable questions. They often fear the presence of an object, even in its absence (unlike phobia). In other words, they have a permanent hesitancy as a personality trait.

Finally, the obsessive is often very orderly, logical and scrupulous, in order to effectively counter his objects of fear.

What are the unconscious mechanisms of these curious symptoms? The obsessive neurotic spends his time performing rituals, in thought or in action, to chase away his anxiety. This one is not linked to the body, as in hysteria, but to thoughts. It originates from an unconscious conflict between the superego and the id. Like any neurotic, the obsessive has a very repressive superego, resulting from a positive Oedipus complex. Killing the father, on the one hand, and loving the mother, on the other hand, are classic. Aggressiveness and sexuality are at their source. But a third element is added to it, resulting from the anal stage. A desire of dirtiness is going to contaminate, it is the case to say it, the sexuality and the usual aggressiveness in the unconscious. To prevent the rise of these repressed motions to consciousness, or even worse to avoid carrying out these reprehensible acts, the neurotic obsessive carries out his absurd rituals. These occupy his attention by diverting it from bad thoughts.

The possibilities are numerous and well known. They are often rituals of cleanliness (to counteract the desires of dirtiness), with an obsession for purity, for fear of contamination. The obsessive neurotic is very superstitious, he is afraid of contagion. A taboo thought risks to contaminate another one, and the chain of these proscribed ideas does not cease lengthening, from where innumerable rituals "anti-taboos". The obsessive neurotic tries to lock himself in an ivory tower so as not to be touched by defilement, the desire for violence and deviant sexuality. Since these bad thoughts are particularly likely to arise at bedtime, bedtime brings a peak of ritual activity.

As for the paranoid, the obsessional is very marked by the anal stage. However, the pleasure taken in defilement is restrained by a tyrannical superego in the obsessive, whereas the paranoid delights in expressing it outwardly, with a filthy and derogatory aggressiveness.

The rituals of politeness result from the latent hostility of obsessive neurotics. They are particularly kind, polite, attentive, and scrupulously respect the many little rituals of social life. In short, they are obedient. They like to have rules prescribed for them to follow.

Finally, they cannot contain a certain pleasure for anything that is repeated, like children. This is their response to the incessant activity of unconscious drives.

Christians are found behind these pathological traits. Their love of rituals is obvious, with their sign of the cross, their "Ave Maria", their host, their "Amen", etc. They show great obedience to traditions, symbolizing the father, as a reaction to the anguishing bad conscience of the desire to kill him and his family. They show a great obedience to traditions, symbolizing the father, as a reaction to the anguishing bad conscience of the desire to kill and demean him. Their superego shows itself all the more tyrannical as their unconscious aggressiveness towards the father is great. Thus, they have a tendency for "purifying" rituals, which wash away their faults, relieving their bad conscience. This permanent guilt makes them appreciate the repetitive recitations of prayers to be performed, after having confessed, as a way of forgiveness. Purity is to be taken literally as well as figuratively: not to soil and not to commit a fault. But the two meanings come together, since one of their most pressing unconscious desires consists of an impulse to defile, inherited from the anal stage. Their desire for purity can never be satisfied: it is a fight against an unconscious tendency, not real acts.

For Christians, sexuality is another source of permanent bad conscience. They consider it impure. Initially, the first impure act is incest. Then, by psychic contagion, almost any sexual act becomes forbidden, dirty, etc. Christians spend a lot of time trying to contain sexuality, trying to channel it within the narrow confines of ever stricter codes. Yet Jesus did not say much about this issue. Except, it is true, to forbid the divorce that Moses had accepted. Jesus was often in good company, defending one adulteress or praising another who washed his feet[220]. Insofar as he was charismatic, and perfectly free from moral laws that did not come from him, to suppose that he had a good time is not unreasonable. No one would throw a stone at him. Except for the evangelists, who no doubt dutifully censored such deviations in their writings, not to mention the other stories set aside by the Christian Church. It doesn't matter, only the fact that the selected texts enjoin a restriction of sexual life to the strict framework of marriage, to see Christians hastening to follow these rules. Or at least try to.

---

220. *Luke* (7: 44-47, 50).

The last source of bad conscience lies in aggressiveness. It is striking to see Christians always so concerned with politeness, attention to others, apparent calm, exaggerated kindness, ostensible thoughtfulness, etc. Too much emphasis on friendliness hides something else, namely its strict opposite. Underneath the excessive efforts of the ego, the hyper-aggressiveness, unconscious, of the obsessive neurotic smoulders. This one appears directly at the time to rectify the wrongs of the others, to make the moral, to preach the good word, etc. As for peace, so dear to Christians, it is well worth it within their circle, but its less glorious counterpart is the war of the crusaders and the delirium of the inquisitors. In short, too many signs of modesty betray a pride and a self-love that grow in secret. The priests, the parish priests, etc., play a comedy to themselves, full of vanity, making a thousand efforts to appear modest and gentle, while the careerists make their way through the Church. The psychologist immediately sees, through this ardor, a beautiful unconscious dose of aggressiveness and pretension (to hold the truth about the ultimate mysteries).

At this point, we have the mechanisms of the very particular personality of Jesus on the one hand, and of his listeners on the other. Let us confront the two to understand how this encounter could have generated a new religion. In psychological terms, it is to understand how the meeting of a megaparanoid with a crowd of obsessive neurotics and hysterics could generate such a success, a real love at first sight. It is a love marriage between madmen. Here is the hour of the fatal kiss.

The problem is twofold. It consists in explaining the birth of this religion, without resorting to the existence of God. It also lies in the fact that it has endured through the generations, long after the death of its instigator.

There are three main types of reasons for this. First, this love affair had to do with the kinds of personalities involved. Second, the content of Jesus' teaching was likely to resonate in the subconscious of his listeners. Third, the form of Jesus' assertions was very convincing, insofar as it largely anticipated modern propaganda.

First, then, let's talk about the fatal attraction between two highly complementary personality types, like the plus and minus poles of two magnets. Jesus had an inverted superego, loving his ego instead of tyrannizing it, to the point of fusion. However, most men have a super-ego which functions normally, as a moral conscience which orders and limits the self. Sometimes, with the neurotics, the superego makes too much, generating anguish and feeling of pathological guilt. Many consequences follow from this configuration on the personality traits of the two groups of protagonists, Jesus and his believers. Jesus rightly called the latter his "sheep". The other translation of this word, "sheep", amounts to the same thing, with the addition of a tender docility that makes the situation worse.

Jesus behaved like a father, his sheep like children, Jesus did not have a guilty conscience, his sheep were tetanized by their sense of guilt, Jesus was certain of holding the truth, his sheep suffered from always doubting, Jesus had a perfectly unique behavior, his sheep imitated each other, Jesus liked to command, his sheep liked to obey, Jesus loved himself, his sheep did not love themselves, Jesus never hesitated, his sheep always hesitated, Jesus liked to right the wrongs of others, his sheep liked to blame themselves, Jesus instituted new rituals, his sheep loved rituals, Jesus was certain that he was pure and could purify mankind, his sheep felt dirty, Jesus had a strong personality, his sheep did not, Jesus was both hateful and loving toward others while loving himself, his sheep turned their hate on themselves and lacked love,

Jesus was overflowing with energy, his sheep were held back by their moral scruples, Jesus was constantly rehashing his delusional ideas, his sheep loved repetition, Jesus had a loving relationship with the archetypal father, his sheep had the guilty conscience of unconsciously hating their father, Jesus invented meaning in the world, his sheep were hungry for meaning, Jesus claimed to act on the world through thought, his sheep were fascinated by occult forces, Jesus represented a model of internal happiness, his sheep were gnawed by anguish, Jesus was persuaded that all eyes were on him, the sheep confusedly aspired to the coming of a liberator, Jesus flattered himself, his sheep criticized themselves, Jesus made mythical projections, his superstitious sheep liked to be able to explain the universe, to know the meaning of life and to guide their actions from myths that it was reassuring to believe...

Sheep existed in Jesus' time, but they have always existed and probably always will. Insofar as Jesus' personality was immortalized in the writings of his admirers, this love marriage between fools was made to last. And they had many children.

The personality of Jesus filters largely through the writings reporting his words and actions. The readers of the Gospels feel it confusedly. Their unconscious perceives it immediately and precisely. Finally, the icing on the cake is that the content of Jesus' words was not only about the specific situation of a Jewish community under Roman occupation. This content was derived from mythical projections, from unconscious relationships, identical for all... All men can believe in the truth of Jesus' claims. His words, if not true in terms of reality, are at least true in terms of the structures of the unconscious, common to all members of the human race.

The main content of Jesus' speeches was his "good news". This was not the resurrection. The resurrection was only a particular case of a more general hope. Let us put aside the fact that there was no real resurrection, but perhaps at best a little accident of Roman procedure, which would have left a few more days of survival for a crucified man who was released too soon. The resurrection would have meant that death was defeated, which is precisely an impression coming from the atemporal id. Jesus would have benefited from a simple combination of circumstances: his poorly executed execution would have provided a semblance of confirmation to his original unconscious conviction.

The resurrection was only a special case of the good news in general. The fundamental workings of the megaparanoid mind is to believe that its unconscious mechanisms are valid in reality. The good news, "forgiveness," was in its own way an incredible novelty. No one had yet made such a precise and insistent mythical projection from this most banal of parental functions. In psychological terms, Jesus was simply projecting his own unconscious ego-superego relationship in a big way: he had no guilty conscience, he felt innocent and pure. He had achieved in his inner self what, metaphorically speaking, could be called a reconciliation with the father (with the superego). It constituted an immense internal liberation. Jesus signed there his most beautiful mythical projection, which would earn him his greatest posterity of megaparanoid, by attributing to God and humanity this same internal relation which governed his superego and his self. All would be forgiven like himself. This is the good news. What happiness to believe in the reality of this improbable unconscious configuration, for neurotics who always have bad conscience!

For the sheep, certainly, not to be torn by the feeling of fault would be a priceless relief. So, for them, they might as well deny the reality, the sordid reality of a life devoid of meaning, filled with psychological suffering and closed by a certain and final death. It was better for them to believe in the myth of an eternal and happy life. It was all the easier for them to give in to it because they felt that there was something true in Jesus' promise, something obscurely true, extremely true, eternally true. There was indeed something true... of the unconscious.

It was the case of the promised eternity in heaven, and well valid, but of the unconscious. This megaprojection was as valid for Jesus' contemporaries as for people of all times. With this promise, Jesus made his interlocutors bathe in his dream, in his unconscious universe - a real bath of eternity.

The promise of social reversal was in the same direction. All men of modest means unconsciously wish to kill their superiors. How happy the underprivileged are to be told that the last will be first! All reversals of the social order, as a return to the golden age, give pleasure to the suffering. The golden age represents itself, like paradise, an era without suffering, without ego-on-ego tension, a fantasized return to primary narcissism. For the neurotics, this golden age is equivalent to the death of the father, in other words to the end of the prohibition of desires. As a bonus, the destructive desires, common to all, are satisfied there. The idea of revolt always pleases the sheep who have turned their aggression on themselves. Here again, Jesus proposed an inner liberation, making them believe that it would be realized in reality (of paradise).

In the same way, men would like to benefit from a paternal protection, as in childhood. Freud had detected in this wish a powerful motor of religion[221]. But sheep are always worried about the future, continually fearing some real misfortune that will punish them, thus confirming the bad conscience that constantly

---

221. See FREUD (Sigmund), "The Future of an Illusion", chapter VI, in *Complete Works. Psychoanalysis*, Paris, PUF, 1994, volume XVIII, p. 170, and also "Malaise in culture", chapter I, p. 258.

CHAPTER VI: OBSESSIVE NEUROTIC SHEEP

plagues them. Jesus gave them the greatest good, announcing that there would be nothing more to fear, that all would be forgiven, and that all would obtain eternal life... on the simple condition that they obeyed him, which confirmed their infantile situation. This would remain effective through the centuries, as long as the sheep did not understand the purely psychological origin of this universal father.

And also, and above all, Jesus proposed to wash away sins. Promising purity to obsessive neurotics could only arouse their greatest enthusiasm. On the one hand, absolute purification, on the other, eternal unconscious guilt: true love was assured.

Jesus fascinated all the sheep of all times. He fascinated them with structures of the unconscious, which he projected into pleasure-provoking myths. Jesus also fascinated them with his personality, a kind of wild beast without internal tension. The good news was embodied in a historical figure. Through admiring identification, the sheep could believe in the end of internal suffering. They let Jesus into their superego. They not only got an internal guide, but also the liberating but illusory sensation of being able to be like him. The good news spread through all those with a sickly superego.

Finally, Jesus' oratory style was, fortunately for him, extremely appropriate for crowds.

To begin with, on the political level, Jesus used some very effective strings. He seduced the little people, who were more psychologically malleable. Simple minds are often more vulnerable to the magnetism of strong personalities. However, the turning point of the case was that the little people, by uniting, became stronger. They were able to impose their views on their former superiors, at least those who were neurotic. The herd instinct of the sheep assured them a new strength, that of numbers, as Nietzsche analyzed[222]. Their perspective, in time, became the dominant illusion.

In order to reach the people, Jesus resorted to unlimited demagogy, insofar as he promised absolutely everything to those who had absolutely nothing. He did not take many risks, and few of them came back from the dead to confirm the validity of his promises. The after-sales service was not overwhelmed. In addition to happiness and eternal life, Jesus offered them a social reversal, which was particularly attractive to those at the bottom of the ladder.

Before the people, Jesus used short, easy-to-understand sentences.

"[...] there will be one flock, one shepherd."[223]

The structure of this sentence is disturbingly reminiscent of this other one: "*Ein Volk, ein Reich, ein Führer*" ("one people, one empire, one leader"). Simple phrases appeal to the simple-minded. But the more people there are in a crowd, the less they think. Jesus knew how to target his speech to his type of listeners.

Then Jesus repeated the same ideas over and over again, with phrases like "I tell you the truth. Sheep love repetitive rituals, like children. Goebbels noted that if you repeat a false idea over and over again, it will eventually be accepted as true. Even today, some heads of state, seeking to pass off a lie, are inspired by this technique, the number of repetitions being proportional to its degree of falsity.

Jesus also had the idea of employing intermediaries, just as a businessman hires employees, who will work in the same direction as him:

---

222. *See* La Généalogie de la morale.
223. *John* (10:16).

"[...] the Lord appointed seventy more disciples, and sent them two by two before him into every city and place where he himself was to go."[224]

By delegating his powers, a boss multiplies his own power of action. Jesus, as a calculating businessman, knew how to sell himself effectively. He trained, directly or indirectly, the cohort of his disciples, apostles, evangelists, fathers of the Church, high ranking ecclesiastics, etc. This process worked all the better with sheep who believed in the contagion of the supernatural. In reality, Jesus was giving them some of his incredible confidence in himself. In turn, they tried to behave like him, like a father who had reversed the ego/self relationship. This was the case of all the Christian leaders, like the fathers of the Church or the Pope, simple paranoiacs having taken over the myths invented by their megaparanoid master.

In addition, Jesus used the effects of hearsay admirably. His own listeners became his most fervent ambassadors, since a satisfied customer is the best assurance of a good reputation. This was eminently the case with hysterics. A good dose of self-confidence cured them, and in addition they were particularly noisy socially, with their constant comedy.

A final tip, to please the masses, is more difficult to achieve. You have to make a nice exit. To know not only how to go out at the top of one's glory, before sadly fading like everyone else, but preferably with a final flourish. To give your life is ideal. People are always impressed by martyrs. They immediately identify with someone who suffers, since it is their daily lot. Jesus' death was a great benefit to his public image. This banal mechanism still works with today's celebrities. To increase one's aura, it is better to die early! - and if possible, die for a good cause. However,

---

224. *Luke* (10:1).

fanaticism is anything but a proof of truth. Dying for an idea does not prove its validity.

In terms of knowledge, Jesus was unknowingly saying things that always seemed to be true.

First, they were so vague and general that they could be applied to any situation, as in astrology. The phrase "seek and ye shall find" can be applied to a job search as well as to a baguette at the bakery. The metaphorical level is even worse. It can refer to truth, faith, God, the meaning of an obscure parable of Jesus, etc.

Then a statistical effect comes into play. In the two millennia that billions of people have been trying to verify these phrases, there are always cases where they work. This makes Jesus look like a great visionary. But this is to consciously forget the other billions of cases where the same sentences have not been verified at all. The statement "from those who have nothing, even what they have will be taken away" can still be applied to bankers who take money from the poor in one way or another. The condition is that all the aid given to the poor, which obviously contradicts the sentence in question, is passed over. This is the mechanism of proverbs, which can always be applied to certain situations, consciously leaving aside the many more where they do not apply.

Jesus' statements were, for the most part, stated in the imperative mode. A command is never true or false. Astrologers know this well, with their supposed predictions of the form "tomorrow, be careful with affection". The facts are not likely to contradict this kind of statement, which is apparently confirmed regardless of the events of the following day. To want to obey the order is enough to have the impression that it is true.

Another more subtle effect gives Jesus' sentences an appearance of truth. His statements become true because they are believed. He said, "Heaven and earth will pass away, but my words will not."[225] All his listeners wanted this statement to come true. It has come true. If a sports team wants to win a game, it must believe that it will win. Without this, success cannot happen. Jesus, by dint of finding himself superior, ended up being believed by all, and he really did become so. It is by believing *a priori* in success that we can bring it about.

A final mechanism, the most devious of all, accounts for the apparent veracity of Jesus' statements. They have "become true" because Jesus' delusional system has become the standard and criterion of truth. From the moment the Christian puts on the glasses of Jesus, everything seems to confirm him, everything being interpreted from his a priori. The Christian thinks that banging his foot against the edge of the bed means that he is being punished by God, whereas he is being punished by his superego. Every event seems to confirm the existence of God, this being presupposed even before interpreting any fact.

Overall, to know if a sentence of Jesus is true, we should not look at the reality. Many situations will always arise to confirm or deny it. To find out if his statements are true, we must look to the unconscious. Jesus teaches us nothing about reality, but a great deal about his unconscious structures, without his knowledge. From these structures he was shaping reality. In doing so, he imposed new appearances on reality. It was a permanent hallucination.

This great appearance of continuous truths, stated in a convincing way, has contributed a lot to its incredible success.

In short, Jesus started out as a mass delusion and then convinced the masses. Freud writes, "It is as such a mass delusion that we must also characterize the religions of humanity."[226]

---

225. *Matthew* (24:35), see also *Mark* (13:31) and *Luke* (21:33).
226. FREUD (Sigmund), "Malaise in Culture", in *Complete Works. Psychoanalysis, op. cit.* Volume XVIII, p. 268.

Jesus was not a shepherd. Jesus was a wolf. Jesus ate the souls of his sheep. He swallowed them up.

After understanding how Jesus' deleterious charisma could have influenced the crowd, a big problem remains, which has emerged in the meantime. What his sheep repeat and follow is not at all what Jesus was, given his pathological symptoms. He did not have the qualities he demanded, quite the contrary. Although fascinated by Jesus' statements, because of their collective unconscious content, how could the neurotics follow both his words and his example? Implicitly, the personality of Jesus was in clear contradiction with what he said.

How could the sheep believe that Jesus had the qualities he demanded? How could he pass for the model of his statements of principle, when he was the real antithesis of them?

CHAPTER VII:
THE CONTRADICTIONS OF JESUS

> Then Jesus, speaking to the crowd and to his
> disciples, said, "The scribes and the Pharisees
> sit in Moses' chair. Do therefore and observe all
> that they say to you; but do not do according
> to their works. For they say, and do not do."
>
> Matthieu[227]

And did Jesus do what he said?

His numerous contradictions represent a privileged access to the complexity of his personality. They allow us to touch the fundamental particularity of this very rare disease that constitutes megaparanoia.

A first series of contradictions is characteristic in this respect, and lies in the gap between what Jesus ordered others to do and what he himself did. Here are a few samples.

---

227. *Matthew* (23:1-3), see also *Luke* (11:45-47).

With his parable of the mote and the beam[228], Jesus enjoined us not to look at the defects of others, but at our own. But this parable is a reproach to others, when he himself had none. More generally, he considered himself innocent, and spent his life righting the wrongs of others. He gave laws to others, while he freed himself from those coming from outside. He did not integrate the law of the father, while projecting his beam into the eye of others.

In this sense, Jesus ordered not to judge, while spending time doing so, especially with those who did not follow him:

"He who believes in him is not judged; but he who does not believe is already judged, because he has not believed in the name of the only Son of God."[229]

Moreover, Jesus was convinced that he was right:

"[...] if I judge, my judgment is true [...]"[230]

Jesus ordered not to lie[231]. But has there ever been a worse liar who promised eternal life, happiness for all, a hundred times what has been given, etc.? His promises were never verifiable, so he never had to account for them.

"Whatever you ask in faith through prayer, you will receive."[232]

Jesus commanded obedience. Yet he spent his life disobeying, not respecting customs, moral laws, the authority of the teachers, etc. He demanded order, imposed by him, without respecting the order, imposed by others. He demanded order, imposed by him, without respecting the order imposed by others. He demanded purity, refusing to behave properly among the Pharisees.

Jesus also commanded to love the father:

---

228. *Matthew* (7:3).
229. *John* (3:18).
230. *John* (8:16).
231. *Matthew* (19:18).
232. *Matthew* (21:21-22).

146

"This is the first: Hear, O Israel, the Lord our God is the only Lord; and: You shall love the Lord your God with all your heart, with all your soul, with all your mind, and with all your strength. The second is: You shall love your neighbor as yourself. There is no other commandment greater than these. [...] Jesus, seeing that he had answered with understanding, said to him, "You are not far from the kingdom of God."[233]

But did Jesus have any merit in loving God the Father if he claimed to be one with him? He loved himself. This is the autophilia of a Trinity whose love is realized in a vacuum.

As for loving others, this is one of Jesus' most famous commands:

"A new commandment I give to you: love one another; as I have loved you, so you also should love one another."[234]

He showed little love to the scribes, the chief priests, the temple merchants, the teachers, the priests, the Pharisees, and finally the Judas of betrayal, to whom he wished he had not been born[235]. Worse, Jesus provoked, insulted and even attacked all those who did not believe in him, whom he called "unbelievers" or "fools". He had a hateful attitude towards those who did not obey him. He was cold to his mother and brothers[236]. On this last point, let us note that his inverted Oedipus led him to love his father.

Incidentally, Jesus' authoritarian personality was not helped by an insidious paradox: love cannot be ordered. To encourage love, the use of orders is somewhat incongruous, and the use of force even more so.

Jesus commanded forgiveness. However, at the moment when he would have had the most opportunity to set an example, he

---

233. *Mark* (12:29-31, 34), see also *Matthew* (22:37-40).
234. *John* (13:34).
235. *Matthew* (26:24).
236. *Luke* (8:19-21).

allowed himself to be invaded by the gall of resentment, as the Judas episode revealed[237]. It is also surprising to see Jesus encouraging denunciation...[238]

He criticized the vanity of others:

"The scribes and Pharisees] love to be greeted in the public places and to be called by men Rabbi, Rabbi. But do not call yourselves Rabbi; for one is your teacher, and you are all brothers. And call no one on earth your father; for one is your Father, he who is in heaven. Do not be called directors; for one is your Director, Christ."[239]

But he was flattered to be called the son of God, and he allowed imitators to do so when it contributed to his own reputation. The preceding quotation also doubles the point, revealing the implicit contradiction of forbidding to call anyone "father" or "director" except himself.

Jesus also commanded that he should not seek glory. Yet he said that his words would not pass muster, and he used many demagogic devices to establish his authority over the crowd.

Jesus identified himself with God, boasted of holding the truth, justice, the key to happiness for all, and claimed to save humanity. On the other hand, he exhorted the crowds to humility, comparing man to dust. Much has been made of the miracles of Jesus, while unjustly overlooking the feat of demanding modesty when one considers oneself to be the son of God.

Regarding self-control, Jesus said:

"You have heard that it was said to the elders: You shall not kill; he who kills shall be liable to judgment. But I say to you that whoever is angry with his brother is liable to judgment [...]"[240]

---

237. See *Matthew* (26:24), *Mark* (14:21), *Luke* (22:22).
238. *Matthew* (18:17).
239. *Matthew* (23:7-10).
240. *Matthew* (5:21-22).

148

What other feeling could have inspired Jesus to destroy the merchants' tables? Angry people always answer that the situation justifies their anger...

Jesus, who often used insults, warned those around him against using them:

"Let him who says to his brother, 'Raca [stupid]!' deserve to be punished by the Sanhedrin [supreme court of the Jews]; and let him who says to him, 'Fool!' deserve to be punished by the fire of Gehenna [eternal punishment]."[241]

He created many enemies, and his relationship with them is also an antinomy:

"But I say to you, do not resist the wicked. If anyone strikes you on the right cheek, turn to him the other also. If someone wants to plead against you and take your tunic, let him have your cloak also. If anyone forces you to go one mile, go two with him. Give to him who asks you, and do not turn away from him who wants to borrow from you."[242]

One should not resist the wicked. But Jesus fled and hid when he knew he was wanted[243]. He claimed to give power to walk on the power of the enemy[244]. In fact, he constantly harassed the scribes and Pharisees, whom he called "wicked".

Jesus ordered not to swear:

"But I say to you, do not swear at all, not by heaven, because it is the throne of God; not by the earth, because it is his footstool; not by Jerusalem, because it is the city of the great king. Neither swear by the head, for you cannot make one hair white or black.

---

241. *Matthew* (5:22).
242. *Matthew* (5:39-42).
243. *Matthew* (12:14-15), (2:22), *Mark* (7:24), (9:30), *John* (7:1), (7:10-11), (11:53-54).
244. *Luke* (10:19).

Let your word be yes, yes, no, no; whatever is added to it is from the evil one."[245]

And the fact is that he hardly swore at all. But the main delusion of Jesus was his identification with God. To forbid swearing, under these conditions, was to prevent insulting him personally. This mechanism would illustrate how an order with a universal claim is created out of his personal psychology, especially his own susceptibility and sense of persecution. That Jesus would finally do what he commanded is no longer surprising. He would have had some difficulty in swearing against himself, especially in view of the love he had for his person.

This list, which is not exhaustive, can be closed with a generalization that makes the heart of the psychological problem clear. Jesus ordered us not to do to others what we would not want them to do to us. Would he have enjoyed meeting another Jesus? Would he have liked to be insulted, assaulted, violated, and told at every moment what he should do, believe, think? Such is the paradox of the paranoid: a being who is extremely sensitive to the hostility of others, and who does not realize his own aggressiveness.

However, Jesus was not a simple paranoid: with him, the paradox goes up a notch. Exploring this difficulty in its ultimate consequences allows us to better understand the specificity of Jesus, through the characteristics of his relationship with others.

All the contradictions of Jesus between his words and his actions have a common source. It is again and again his inverted superego that made him create laws and direct his reproachful aggressiveness towards others, never towards himself. Being at the origin of laws, he exempted himself from them, while imposing them on those around him.

---

245. *Matthew* (5:34-37).

A serious problem arises for his sheep, which is characteristic of their master's very special pathology. These sheep would love to follow a character who seems to know what he is talking about. Two contradictory solutions are presented to them. Either follow Jesus in action, and question the content of his words. Or follow Jesus' words, and question Jesus in action, as a model of life.

The greatest paradox of Christianity appears, very revealing of the personality of its initiator: following Jesus is impossible. However, billions of men thought they could do it...

Let us not forget the love marriage between Jesus and his sheep. They wanted to follow him, and he wanted to be followed:

"[...] I have given you an example, that you may do as I have done to you."[246]

But his life is the exact opposite of what he ordered to be done. How could his sheep follow maxims contradicted by actions? How could they follow someone whose personality was the antithesis of what he demanded of his sheep? How could they continue to believe in the divinity of such a contradictory being? How to take as a model a being so inconsistent in his approach? How to follow an inconsistent approach ?

Jesus' sheep have an important dilemma to solve, without being aware of it: should they follow Jesus' example, i.e. his actions, or his teaching?

Let's try to consider the first way.

An astonishing contradiction immediately appears. If they had really imitated Jesus' actions, the sheep would have, like him, destroyed the stalls of the merchants in the temple, like the commercial products sold at Lourdes. To generalize, since Jesus was poor and critical of accumulated wealth, the sheep would have ransacked the colossal fortune amassed by the

---

246. *John* (13:15).

Christian Church over the past two thousand years. It would never have amassed such wealth, the same Church that claims to be Jesus'...

She opted for the other choice, following him in his teaching, not in his actions. Let us examine this second path. If the Church is not feasible in the purity of its idea, is it feasible in its human characterization?

The solution might be to obey the words of Jesus. These words are in themselves relatively coherent, even if their starting point is delusional. Frank contradictions arise again.

To follow his precepts to the letter, the sheep would have to ignore the actions of Jesus. This is difficult. His teaching contains the very advice to imitate him.

Immediately a second problem arises, which is to be blind to the actions of Jesus. This problem has been solved historically, albeit at the expense of the truth. It was solved by forming a false idea of Jesus. He has a false reputation among his sheep. They see him with the glasses he invented. They imagine him with the values he imposed. Jesus demanded humility, so the sheep believe him to be modest. He castigated hypocrisy and lies, so the sheep believe him to be frank and honest. He imposed love, so the sheep believe him to be kind. And so on. In doing so, the sheep do not look at him with the right glasses. They hallucinate him. They see him with qualities that were not his. In addition to seeing him differently than he was, they blind themselves to what he really was. The sheep operate a kind of internal and permanent censorship on the many psychological characteristics of Jesus. The paradox is striking: his own character traits were the very flaws he was castigating.

This is the solution for believing in following Jesus: to veil the true image of what he was in action, of what he did. The sheep put on the glasses of his words, and confuse him with the ideal world he portrayed. This is the way they can get a false idea of him. To follow only his injunctions, they must see him through the values of his sentences. And they confuse the man Jesus with the ideal he professed. At the cost of an immense hallucination about Jesus himself, the sheep can believe they are following both his words and his example.

All these complications allow us to approach the goal: to determine as closely as possible the psychological particularities of the man Jesus and to understand his success, by means of the imbroglios that cannot fail to generate the meeting of a megaparanoid with the many neurotics.

Assuming that the major discrepancies between Jesus' words and deeds are resolved without hallucinations, the supreme contradiction will never be resolved. After the first great discrepancy, between his words and his deeds, comes a second, even more radical contradiction. His words and actions were one thing, but his personality was another.

In other words, there is saying, doing and being.

Can we follow Jesus in his very being?

The first problem arises immediately: having this or that personality is not something you choose. No one chooses to be a psychotic, let alone a megaparanoid like Jesus. Not even Jesus. "Not just anyone can become crazy."[247]

A fortiori, a humble sheep could not imitate a formidable megaparanoid.

Let us suppose that this is possible, or rather that the person who would want to follow the actions of Jesus already has the same personality as him. Another insurmountable difficulty arises: such a person would not put himself in the position

247. Lacan (Jacques), *Propos sur la causalité psychique*, Bonneval, 1946.

Chapter VII: The Contradictions of Jesus

of a sheep, by definition. He would not seek to imitate. In other words, if a new Jesus came along, he would not follow Jesus. Just as Jesus did not follow Moses. In short, the one who would be like Jesus would not follow his predecessors, especially Jesus.

Jesus' being was defined by opposition to the actions of others. This being resided in his megaparanoia, which included the delirious need to contradict any laws about what to do or not to do. The essence of Jesus, his very being, consisted in constantly questioning the ethical-religious precepts. How to follow this principle, without immediate contradictions?

Jesus reproached the Pharisees for serving God only in appearance, by keeping to strict ritual obedience. This same reproach can easily be transferred directly to later Christians, who are themselves hypocritical and conceited, and who show up in church praying ostentatiously.

When such a megaparanoid gives a new order, it is impossible to follow it. This is the paradox of Jesus, his very being. To truly follow Jesus as a model, the sheep would have to give new orders to themselves and to others. This would be Jesus in the flesh. It would not be Jesus in verb, in its literal content.

The very principle of a Christian Church is contradictory. It freezes the orders of Jesus, their content. In so doing, it contradicts its very being, which challenges the fixed orders. The idea of the Church being incoherent, its attempts at human realization could only generate aberrations.

The fathers and doctors of the Church played on this contradiction. On the one hand, they wanted to impose the content of the doctrine of Jesus, by freezing it. This was a betrayal of Jesus as a model. On the other hand, they slightly modified the content of this doctrine. This was betraying Jesus in his words, while remaining faithful to his principle, to his being. In both cases, they served as a sounding board for Jesus' delusion.

The case of Augustine is interesting. This saint was obsessed with sexuality. In his youth, and in accordance with Roman customs, he had joyfully indulged in orgies. But then Augustine the orgiast was struck by the teaching of Jesus. If he had been touched by the spirit of Jesus, he should not have had a guilty conscience. He would simply have taught that one should practice debauchery, inventing a Jesus-like justification, such as "God is love, make love". The Cathars, otherwise known as the "Pure Ones," had a similar revelation, taking the astonishing step of enacting Jesus' sense of innocence through incessant feasts that celebrated the joys of the body. But Augustine had been impressed by the content of Jesus' teaching, which reduced sexuality to the bare minimum of marriage (and even then within very narrow limits). Augustine exaggerated these drastic restrictions to the point of asceticism. By slightly changing the letter of Jesus, he was in keeping with the spirit of Jesus. Other sheep came to follow this new model to the letter. Sheep will always come to observe any teaching, the main thing being to follow rules. The church fathers acted as a sounding board, with a necessary distortion, given the impossibility of following both the spirit of Jesus and his letter. To these problems are added the inevitable schisms, the parables of Jesus being vague, always subject to a thousand interpretations.

In short, the contradictions between being, doing and saying of Jesus are inevitably found in the religious practice of sheep. But they do not bother the sheep. To believe in the truth of Jesus' sentences is to prefer the reality of the unconscious to the reality... of reality. Only the "real reality" does not suffer contradictions. The unconscious doesn't care.

CHAPTER VII: THE CONTRADICTIONS OF JESUS

In order to be overwhelmed by the unconsciousness of Jesus, the sheep are content to believe that the mythical beings he projected exist in reality. From then on, all the real facts are interpreted from these glasses. And the most beautiful, Jesus himself.

Conclusion

Jesus said to them, "What do you know about me? Truly, I say to you, no generation of those who are among you will know me."

Judas

The modern atheist had great difficulty in explaining the origin of Jesus' words and deeds, and even more so his success with the crowds in his time and for two millennia. The problem was compounded by the fact that a large part of the European population declares itself to be an atheist, while still following most of the teachings of Jesus, often without realizing it.

The solution which is imposed, after psychological analysis of his symptoms, consists in seeing in Jesus a madman; more precisely, a psychotic with an anal character, that is to say a paranoid, with his systematized deliriums; and more exactly still, a megaparanoid, in other words a madman whose deliriums are built with the materials of the collective unconscious. He made mythical projections, which fascinate the crowds of neurotics. He captivated them all the more because he projected this internal relation of love of oneself, of reconciliation ego-on-ego, which characterized his own unconscious. This extraordinary megaprojection could only bewitch the neurotics, whose psychological structure resides in a painfully guilt-ridden opposition between ego and super-ego. This fact is accentuated for the obsessive neurotics, who sickly need rites based on myths. These neurotics believe in spirits acting on matter. They believe in a mythical universe to explain the real world. They are convinced that they can influence the course of events through their prayers and magical rituals. But these magical actions only serve to soothe their own pathological anguish. In the same way, those other particular neurotics, who express this pathological tension through their bodies, i.e. the hysterics, were especially susceptible to being impressed by a megaparanoid like Jesus. The latter was a real walking superego. Thanks to his charisma, he acted directly on the unconscious of the hysterics, as if by a natural hypnosis. Once he had entered the unconscious of his patients, Jesus could control their physical symptoms.

The meeting between these two types of madmen, the megaparanoid on the one hand and the obsessive neurotics on the other, with the public echo offered by the hysterics, gave birth to Christianity. The first invented mythical beings, the second believed in them. The latter found a strong unconscious interest in it: Jesus allowed them to believe in a "fathering" universe, with a happy end, instead of a life filled with vain sufferings and closed by a death without appeal.

We can summarize the views developed in this book through the following table, marking the progression of this investigation.

After examining Jesus' madness and the origin of his delusions, the question arises: Did Jesus believe in what he was saying? Some modern atheists, desperate to see him as a wise man, claim that his claims about God and heaven were metaphorical. They retranslate his principles, claiming that he actually meant that God is within us - internal happiness then meaning reconciliation with God. On the level of unconscious functioning, a man is certainly happier if he is not tyrannized by his superego. But what was Jesus' point of view?

In order to answer this question, we must ask ourselves about the general motive of his actions. He sought neither political power nor personal wealth. However, it is likely that he could have used his incredible charisma to obtain them to his heart's content. It is also hard to say whether he took advantage of his success to obtain carnal pleasures. If he had been as preoccupied with sexuality as Augustine, at least indirect clues would have filtered through, if only with strict prohibitions on the matter. These three great motives for action, power, money and sexuality, which are typical of people who have left their mark on history, hardly seem to have concerned Jesus.

There is still vanity. It is true that Jesus was extremely vain, to the point of spending his life trying to obtain the approval of the crowds for his own megalomaniacal delusions. But he structured his whole life around his own delusions, not around the often reproving gaze of others. His vanity was only a by-product of his deep enlightenment and his need for aggressive control. Others had to think like him. As Nietzsche said, "... you would like to seduce your neighbor with your love and bask in his error."[248]

Above all, a paranoid never compromises on the truth. It is his very definition to maintain an untruth, his delusion, against everyone's opinion. The truth obsesses him.

---

248. NIETZSCHE (Friedrich), *Thus Spoke Zarathustra*, Part I, "On the Love of Neighbor", Paris, Gallimard, 1947, p. 74.

CONCLUSION

Jesus' main delusion was that he believed he was the son of God. He organized his life around this genuine conviction, at a time when the whole of society believed in the existence of at least one supernatural entity. Even worse, he reinforced this delusion by developing it. This delirious filiation was prolonged by a love relationship with the father, which turned to the fusional identity in the schizophrenic Trinity. His affirmations are to be taken literally.

The fact that he did not derive more concrete benefits from his ascendancy over the crowd, aggravates his case. He did not even connect with reality in its most attractive aspects, when it held out its arms to him. He remained in the skies of his delusions all his life. Some would see in this attitude a proof of his greatness. It was his supreme folly.

The fate of Jesus and of Christianity is played out around this existence, real or only psychic, of God. The believer interprets all events from the idea of God, which gives him the impression that they are only the consequence of divine action, "therefore" its proof. In reality, these same events can be explained today with the discoveries made in the meantime by science. In particular, psychology makes it possible to explain why believers believe in God, and even why Jesus passed for a divine being. Explaining these facts no longer requires recourse to God. Certainly, other phenomena still await explanation by science. This apparent weakness is the strength of science, which prefers to progress slowly in its explanations. It conquers one by one solid discoveries, rather than declaring all knowledge *a priori*, once and for all and from the beginning, as the Bible did, at a time when knowledge was, to say the least, in its infancy.

But the question of the existence of God remains outside the field of reality, and thus of science. God not being visible, the question of his existence remains undecidable, and moreover useless for science. In this sense, God does not exist for science.

But we can see the facts, simply. We can see that a child grows up. His mind, his forms, his beliefs change. It is a necessary, inevitable, inescapable fact: he grows. For his education, he needs at least one adult, who teaches him how to live in society and in nature.

It is the same with humanity. We can see that humanity is growing. Its spirit, its forms, its beliefs are evolving. It is a necessary, inevitable, ineluctable fact: it is growing. In order to act, it now gives itself its own laws, thanks to the pluralism of democracy, instead of resorting to an authoritarian megaparanoid who decided alone what should be done or not. The West calls "progress" the fact of growing up mentally.

During its early childhood, humanity too had needed at least one adult to teach it how to live in nature. It needed a grown-up to reassure it in the face of hostile nature. As long as humanity was infantile, it had to believe in a father. It was God.

The atheists would tire uselessly to refute his existence. All their arguments will be in vain in the face of an irrational faith, which depends in fact on a mental age - an age at which a world without God seems frightening. Believers, like children, need an all-powerful father to guide their actions. This father is like a daydream, which they feel confusedly within them and which they attribute to an invisible reality, heaven. He constitutes a projection of their collective superego, a dreamlike hallucination shared by many. One can well believe, temporarily, in the reality of a dream, but when one wakes up, one knows that one has returned to reality. The believer believes, the atheist knows.

This mental age of believers does not mean that childhood is "inferior" to adulthood: childhood is necessary, just as the end of childhood is necessary. Humanity grows, naturally. The need for a father disappears by itself, as childhood and its evanescent beliefs disappear. With progress, atheism imposes itself, as a fact, as the inevitable consequence of humanity's coming of age.

Recreation:
Test your Ability to Be a Prophet

In this book we have tried to reconstruct the personality of Jesus from remote writings. We have argued that he was a mega-paranoid. The astonished reader would probably like to verify the validity of this result with facts. Against all expectations, it is possible.

If you want to experience for yourself, *in situ*, the central assertion of this book, go to Africa or the United States, in order to find the level of psychological development as close as possible to the era of the character studied here. There, a host of prophets are active. They found churches with great energy (we say "sect", not "church", the latter having simply succeeded in establishing itself, while the sect tends to do so). You will see these great madmen up close, superb wild beasts, and you will find in them the psychiatric symptoms examined in these lines. You will be able to deduce, by yourselves, the psychological mechanisms which are secretly at work in their enlightened minds. By the way, you will be amused by the wonderful names these churches call themselves, such as "Celestial Christians," "Revival Church," "New Daddy Church," etc.

With a bit of boldness, you could, in turn, start your own church. This is the opportunity for a little game: how to start your own church, to become rich and adored?

Here are some ingredients, as an example:

1/ Absolutely avoid countries that are too used to science, such as England, Germany and France.

2/ Convince investors by your charisma to: buy a big house, have enough to live on and move around. Your future sheep will have to be welcomed for masses. Making rounds to galvanize other sheep also requires means.

3/ Come up with a little idea that is a little different from your colleagues to characterize God's functions. Your product should stand out with some sort of benefit. For example that God's hat is the starry vault, and that your followers must wear big hats to belong to your church. That would be the church of the heavenly hats.

4/ Repeat your new principles over and over, never getting tired of it: "A hat is beautiful, a beautiful hat is a second skin, it's the skin of the Daddy upstairs."

5/ Prepare a very special doctrine about money. You can command to bathe naked in the universe, but wearing a beautiful hat. You sell the hats, and in the symbolic deprivation, you emphasize the importance of not having money, which is dirty. You purify the disciples by taking away their impurities. This money is supposed to provide for the proper functioning of your church, which has the task of spreading the light of your truths.

6/ Prepare initiation rites, with lots of obedience and meaningless assertions. Any rite or statement will have an unconscious meaning anyway. This is the time to let yourself be inspired to express a powerful delusion. If you are a woman, you can present yourself as a universal mother, to symbolize the love of the almighty for all. At the same time, loving the symbol of their mother will give them a boost of unconscious pleasure. You could also announce the imminent return of Jesus. The crowd likes to see familiar names. You take less risk in making a hit with a tune that has already worked. And promises, which can always be delayed, are also an old trick of the trade.

7/ Remember to put in a safe place the money you earn as you go along, the world has no shortage of tax havens. Also, always have a plane ticket on you for the said paradise, which will turn out to be real for at least one member of your church. As soon as the situation turns sour, make a good exit, that's the most important thing. There always comes a time when the earnings curve reaches a ceiling. Know how to get out, without biting off more than you can chew. Make believe you're dead, it's an extra chance to reach posterity, not to mention the open possibility of a future resurrection.

But by the way, now that you know how to start your own church, a business that doesn't suffer from the crisis, there is one last condition to fulfill: do you have the right personality to be a prophet?

To find out, answer the following questions as honestly and lucidly as possible, even if it means recognizing in yourself what Christian morality would call a "flaw". You will know if you are made to be a prophet. After answering the questions, go to the end of the test to calculate the points you scored and the corresponding result.

Question #1: In elementary school, you were more of a:
  A - the band leader ;
  B - a student among others, not especially forward or backward;
  C - the scapegoat, a bit clumsy, on whom all the classmates
      would vent their anger.

Question #2: You tend to feel:
   A - to be often misunderstood, betrayed or victim of an injustice;
   B - to always be perfectly understood;
   C - to have your words distorted only occasionally.

Question 3: Concerning spirits and ghosts:
   A - you don't believe in them and fantasy films tend to bore you;
   B - you believe in it and you are scared to death of it;
   C - you believe in them like hell, but they don't scare you, because you know how to command them.

Question #4: On the topics of conversation that you are passionate about:
   A - you get fired up, you can't stop talking, you argue with endless dialectic, you clarify the meaning of words, you invent words when necessary, and you make metaphors at every turn;
   B - you listen to the conversation with more interest than usual, giving your point of view and listening to that of others;
   C - you drink the words of those who speak well of it, without daring to intervene.

Question 5: When sentences arise in a conversation that go beyond the previous topic:
   A - you let yourself be carried away by the new subject, even if it means changing the subject again, and never returning to the initial subject;
   B - you tend to want to close the parenthesis, and return to the initial subject, to maintain a certain order and logic;
   C - you only come back to the original topic if it was really important, and the main point has not yet been made.

Question #6: Regarding your intimate secrets, you tend to:
   A - don't especially feel pleasure in keeping them to yourself
       or disclosing them;
   B - keep them to yourself, or even use anonymity and
       pseudonyms;
   C - to tell everything and everyone.

Question #7: Regarding controlling your nerves:
   A - you always prefer to try to take on the ambient tensions,
       to calm the game, even if it means wiping the anger of
       others;
   B - you tend to keep your cool, in most circumstances;
   C - you often get carried away or lose your patience.

Question #8: When it comes to the behavior of your loved ones,
   you tend to:
   A - give them a lot of advice when you think they are on the
       wrong track, even when they have not asked you for it;
   B - say nothing, even if you disapprove of their behavior;
   C - sometimes try to make them understand, gently, that they
       are acting against their own interest, when they really are
       making a big mistake.

Question #9: Do you sometimes feel like:
   A - to be the center of interest, to be observed, to be praised
       and admired for your achievements, to be a kind of local
       celebrity;
   B - to be occasionally evoked by others ;
   C - never to interest anyone.

Question #10: When playing a game or sport with a winner and
a loser:
A - you have a keen sense of competition, which gives you the
priority objective of being first, and you prefer to explain
your eventual defeat by your own failures, rather than
concede the slightest credit to your opponent ("it would
hurt you");
B - you have a strong reluctance towards anything that is
competitive or confrontational, and you prefer to lose, if
only to please the winner;
C - you play the game, so much the better if you win, so much
the worse if you lose, you will congratulate the winner.

Question #11: Do you sometimes have new ideas?
A - never, nothing new has crossed your mind;
B - sometimes it happened, but not enough to whip up a cat,
just a find or two;
C - always, and great ideas that could be stolen at any moment,
ideas that could change the course of history, ideas of
grandiose reforms, which allowed you and you alone to
understand everything.

Question #12: Compared to those around you, you feel:
A - similar to others, with a personality of its own, like
everyone else;
B - similar to the others, quite average or even lower ;
C - clearly exceptional, profoundly unique and superior, quite
different.

Question #13: You believe:

A - that bad dreams precede sad events, that meeting a black
cat is a bad sign, and that comets herald misfortunes;

B - that superstition is ridiculous;

C - that many concomitant signs, from the sudden arrival of
good weather to the smile of the concierge, through the
turd in which you planted your shoe, announce without a
doubt your coming consecration.

Question n° 14: In your relationships with your friends, profes-
sional, family or lovers:

A - you are the kind of person who never quarrels with
anyone, always taking it upon yourself to avoid direct
confrontation;

B - there are often disputes, clashes, violent differences of
opinion that are not resolved;

C - apart from a little friction from time to time, you rarely
fall out with others.

Question #15: You observe your own behavior and your own
body:

A - non-stop ;

B - never ;

C - quite often or sometimes.

Question #16: Are you sensitive?

A - no, you readily admit the criticism as justified;

B - a little, like everyone else, but quickly recovered;

C - no, why? The criticism that has been made of you is ridiculous! You'll have to explain yourself in three weeks when
you find the idiot who made it.

RECREATION: TEST YOUR ABILITY TO BE A PROPHET

Question #17: On the subject of insecurity:
   A - you have relative confidence in your country's law enfor-
       cement and authorities, while still fearing that attacks will
       occasionally hit their target;
   B - you have full confidence in the law enforcement agencies
       and authorities of your country;
   C - you do not trust at all the forces of order and the authorities
       of your country, fearing moreover a generalized machina-
       tion, including espionage, conspiracy, defamation, unde-
       rhanded attacks, poisoning, weapons of mass destruction,
       hooks, possibly directed against yourself in person, reason
       for which a constant attention towards others is necessary.

Question #18: In your job or studies, you are more:
   A - ambitious and careerist, ready to take someone else's place
       if necessary, "that's the way society is, you can't help it, it's
       the game";
   B - moderately ambitious, just doing what is necessary to live well;
   C - not at all ambitious, working the bare minimum, or even
       the least possible, as long as the community does not suffer.

Question #19: Do you feel yourself:
   A - modest and simple;
   B - rather proud and confident;
   C - neither of the two.

Question #20: By those around you, you are perceived as:
   A - modest and simple;
   B - rather proud and confident;
   C - neither of the two.

Question n° 21: When you receive a criticism, your first reflex is:
  A - to criticize your interlocutor from the word go, before even
      thinking of examining the criticism he or she is making;
  B - to accept its criticism, by questioning yourself immediately;
  C - to examine his criticism, to see if it is fair.

Question #22: Regarding standards and storage:
  A - you like order, especially when it is imposed with an iron
      hand by active and firm officials; when the light is orange,
      you stop, because it will turn red;
  B - you are not too disorganized, without being maniacal,
      in other words, quite orderly for some things, less so for
      others; at the orange light, you pass ;
  C - you like to have a place for everything in your home
      and everything in its place, to spend no more money
      than is strictly necessary, to make beautiful collections of
      objects that are not necessarily indispensable, to remain
      impassive by controlling your feelings, to make clear and
      well-defined choices without ever coming back to them,
      to program your life over the next fifty years according to
      a brilliant plan, and finally to impose your ordered vision
      of the right course of action on your loved ones; you like
      to honk at people who go through the orange light, and
      you go through the red.

Question #23: Perception question, do you ever:
  A - often being the only one to hear sounds or voices, suspec-
      ting others of being crazy, attributing your own plans or
      intentions to others, attributing your own qualities or
      faults to others, or having deja vu impressions;

B - to have sometimes misunderstood or misseen something,
but to rectify immediately ;
C - to trust people who tell you that they have heard a voice
that you have not heard yourself, they seem to be sure of
their facts.

Question #24: Sexually:
A - you like to dominate, whip, humiliate and bite your
partner's ass;
B - you like to be dominated, to be whipped, to be humiliated
and to have your buttocks bitten;
C - neither, sadomasochism is not your cup of tea.

Question n° 25: Concerning the destiny of humanity:
A - you sometimes have states of daydreaming and intense
excitement, during which you find solutions to all the
problems of the earth, and you feel personally called to
guide humanity to bring these solutions, you who are
certainly the direct descendant of a historical figure and
who are called by the same occasion to enrich yourself
while gleaning a place in the pantheon of men whose
name will be remembered by the peoples forever;
B - you never have such states, but would be inclined to take
seriously someone who would have states of daydreaming
and intense excitement, during which he would see
solutions to all the problems of the earth, and who would
feel personally called to lead humanity to bring these
solutions, he who is most certainly the direct descendant
of a historical figure and who is called at the same time to
enrich himself while gleaning a place in the pantheon of

the men whose names will be remembered by the peoples forever;

C - you let the politicians do their job, especially at the UN, to guide humanity.

Results: Calculate the points you have earned, and read on to find out if you are cut out to be a prophet!

	1	2	3	4	5	6	7	8	9	10	11	12	13	14	15	16	17	18	19	20	21	22	23	24	25
A	2	2	1	2	0	1	0	2	2	2	0	1	0	0	2	0	1	2	2	0	2	0	2	2	2
B	1	0	0	1	2	2	1	0	1	0	1	0	1	2	0	1	0	1	0	2	0	1	1	0	0
C	0	1	2	0	1	0	2	1	0	1	2	2	2	1	1	2	2	0	1	1	1	2	0	1	1

You have less than ten points:

You lost. You are a sheep. You love to be told what to do, you don't like to take the slightest risk or initiative, you always end up last no matter what group you belong to, you are exploited and you don't like it. You just have to hope that the last ones will be the first ones one day.

Conclusion: You should go to a country ruled by a tyrant, his yoke will please you. Or better, go to church.

You have more than forty points:

Congratulations, you've won! You are made to teach the crowds what to do in life! You will be looking for more and more sheep.

"How? Are you looking to multiply yourself by ten, by a hundred? Are you looking for disciples? Then look for *zeros!*"[249]

---

249. NIETZSCHE (Friedrich), *Crépuscule des idoles*, § 14, "Maximes et traits", in *Œuvres philosophiques complètes*, Paris, Gallimard-NRF, 1990, tome VIII, p. 63.

RECREATION: TEST YOUR ABILITY TO BE A PROPHET

Conclusion: You have the material to build your own church. However, keep an eye out for the sirens, which may announce at any moment that there is an ambulance, from which men dressed in white will appear. They are coming for you.

You have between ten and forty points:
You are made to live in a democracy, you are perfectly normal. For you, laws must be chosen democratically, through multilateral decisions. It is men who decide together what is allowed to be done, not a single man inspired by God.
Conclusion: Good luck, and beware of megaparanoids, especially if you are surrounded by sheep.

Table of Contents

Best sellers Max Milo Editions

Hitler's banker, Jean-François Bouchard

Confessions of a forger, Éric Piedoie Le Tiec

The Koran and the flesh, Ludovic-Mohamed Zahed

Governing by fake news, Jacques Baud

Governing by chaos, Collectif

A political history of food, Paul Ariès

Mad in U.S.A.: The ravages of the "American model",
Michel Desmurget

Mondial soccer club geopolitics, Kévin Veyssière

Putin: Game master?, Jacques Braud

Treatise on the three impostors: Moses, Jesus, Muhammad,
The Spirit of Spinoza

TV Lobotomy, Michel Desmurget